Super Easy
PowerXL
AIR FRYER PRO
COOKBOOK

Find quick and effortless recipes for dishes featuring fish, seafood, meat, poultry, pizza, and rotisserie.

JANE M. SMITH

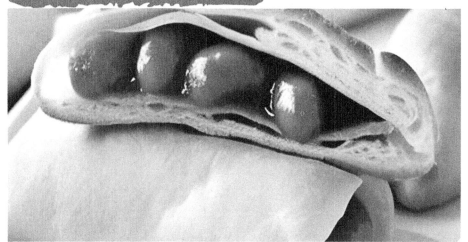

CONTENTS

Cumin Pork Sticks

Bell Pepper Chips

Crunchy Bacon Bites

Broccoli Fries with Spicy Dip

Spicy Dip

Crunchy Broccoli Fries

Cheesy Zucchini Sticks

BBQ Lil Smokies

Baby Corn

Summer Meatball Skewers

Cauliflower Bombs with Sweet & Sour Sauce

Fried Pickle Chips with Greek Yogurt Dip

Old-fashioned Onion Rings

Cashew Dip

Sweet Potato Bites

Roasted Peanuts

Crispy Eggplant

Party Chicken Pillows

Vegetable Mix

Quick and Easy Popcorn

Cheese Dill Mushrooms

Simple Radish Chips

Roasted Parsnip

Apple Chips

Polenta Sticks

Fried Green Tomatoes

Coconut Cookies

Crust-less Meaty Pizza

Spinach Dip

Italian-style Tomato-parmesan Crisps

Cocktail Flanks

Bacon Croquettes

Cheese Bacon Jalapeno Poppers

Grilled Cheese Sandwiches

Cheese Pastries

Pizza Bites

Pineapple Bites with Yogurt Dip

Chocolate Bacon Bites

Avocado Wedges

Saucy Asian Short Ribs

Lemon Tofu

Mexican Muffins

Carrots & Rhubarb

Party Time Mixed Nuts

Curly's Cauliflower

Avocado Fries with Chipotle Sauce

Beef Bites

Tomato & Avocado Egg Rolls

Tomatoes & Herbs

Oliver Fritters

Veggie Bread Rolls

Country-style Deviled Eggs

Chicken Wings in Barbecue Sauce

Spicy Avocado Fries Wrapped in Bacon

Potato Wedges

Ranch Dipped Filets

Mozzarella Snack

Asian Teriyaki Chicken

Ricotta Balls

Pita Bread Cheese Pizza

Brussels Sprouts

Puppy Poppers

Flavorful Pork Meatballs

Veggie Cream Stuff Mushrooms

Onion Dip

Lemon Tofu Cubes

Cheddar Cheese Breadsticks

Easy Habanero Wings

Classic Buttermilk Biscuits

Ninja Pop-tarts

Zucchini Brownies

Avocado Cake

Vanilla Pound Cake

Choco-coconut Puddin

Chocolate Molten Lava Cake

Nuts Cookies

Crème Brulee

Dark Chocolate Brownies

Nutella And Banana Pastries

Orange Swiss Roll

Egg Custard

Creamy Rice Pudding

Peach Parcel

Vanilla Coconut Cheese Cookies

Mom's Orange Rolls

Vanilla Mozzarella Balls

Peach Slices

Butter Crumble

White Chocolate Berry Cheesecake

Coconut Strawberry Fritters

Classic White Chocolate Cookies

Lemon Glazed Muffins

Apple Bread Pudding

Blueberry Pancakes

Lemon Curd

Coconut Chip Cookies

Almond Bars

Rustic Baked Apples

Banana Split

Greek-style Griddle Cakes

Cashew Pie

Ricotta And Lemon Cake Recipe

THANK YOU FOR READING THIS BOOK

INTRODUCTION

What is PowerXL Air Fryer?

With the PowerXL Air Fryer, you can effortlessly prepare flavorful chicken and pig roasts, delectable turkey breasts, and traditional kebabs. Even healthy dehydrated vegetables, herbs, fruit, and other foods can be made with the dehydrator.

RAPID AIR TECHNOLOGY: The PowerXL Air Fryer's Rapid Air Technology surrounds your food with a tornado of turbo cyclonic air to quickly cook it to your preferred level of crispiness without frying it.

7-IN-1 MULTI-COOKER: To replace deep fryers, rotisseries, dehydrators, convection ovens, oven toasters, and pizza grills, super-heated turbo cyclonic air surrounds your food with crisp 360° air circulation. Even a 4-pound chicken can fit in this 1700-watt air fryer oven!

COOK WITH LESS OIL: Compared to deep-fried food, the Power Air FryerXL offers 70% fewer calories from fat. You can enjoy all of the crispy, juicy, tasty, and healthy advantages of oil-free air frying with the PowerXL Air Fryer Pro multi-cooker.

8 PRESET BUTTONS WITH ONE TOUCH: You may roast, air fry, bake, steam, sauté, and grill using 8 computerized pre-set programs that are simple to use with a single touch. offering a manual time and temperature setting option in addition to a digital timer with automatic shutoff

Modern, efficient, and cutting-edge air fryers include the PowerXL. It offers more effective services, enhances food quality, preserves nutrients, and gives our meals a distinctive and alluring aroma. It has eight culinary gadgets that give us the ultimate convenience while preparing food without having to worry about temperature ranges or cooking periods. We can prepare the tastiest food ever in the shortest amount of time by just adding your preferred ingredients, selecting the desired setting, and waiting a short while. One of the best lunchtime helpers ever made, in my opinion. It provides flawless cooking for all of our meals in a lot less time by combining advanced air-crisp technology with a premium, commercial-grade grill plate.

One of the most inventive and cutting-edge kitchen equipment, the PowerXL Air Fryer offers more cooking possibilities and a larger capacity than comparable grills. The device is incredibly sturdy and has a 6-quart capacity despite its small size. The following sections will discuss 12 pre-programmed cooking modes with a temperature range of 180 to 500 degrees Fahrenheit. The PowerXL Air Fryer is the perfect appliance for grilling inside thanks to the attached nonstick grill plate. Vegetables, fruits, fish, and meats may all be grilled with little oil and effort.

No other traditional cooking appliance can compare to the PowerXL Air Fryer's wide variety of adjustable functionalities. The device's wide temperature adjustment range lets you master all of the cooking methods it provides. You can better grasp the equipment, its numerous parts, its basic operations, and how to clean and maintain it with the aid of this manual. Additionally, this cookbook will give you well-written, simple-to-follow recipes to help you make the most of your PowerXL Air Fryer and encourage a healthy lifestyle for you and your loved ones. What benefits does the PowerXL Air Fryer offer?

This part discusses why the PowerXL Air Fryer is the ideal solution for our kitchen needs.

Flexible Cooking Techniques
We can prepare food without anxiety utilizing any recipe, preprogrammed cooking capability, and 12 different cooking methods.

Little to no oil
Utilizing quick air crisp technology, the PowerXL Air Fryer gives our food a crisp, crunchy texture while using little to no oil.

easy cleaning
The majority of the device's parts and components are dishwasher-safe, thus cleaning them is not necessary. Details regarding cleaning and maintenance will be provided in the sections that follow.

Small Size
The equipment is incredibly small and compact, which allows us to free up a lot of kitchen space.

The PowerXL l Air Fryer's principal parts are as follows: It may be easily cleaned with a sponge or damp cloth because it is made of stainless steel. Never immerse it in liquids or water.
Before starting the cooking function, the air-frying lid is connected to the main unit using this, as the process cannot start without it.
Never touch the handle of the lid directly since it could get extremely hot while cooking.
The panel de control has buttons for many different culinary requirements and functions.
Grill Plate: A tool for using the quick-air-crisp cooking method while air-frying. It is fully capable of steaming, warming up, and grilling meats and veggies.
Other parts include a ladle, an inner pot, a glass cover, a control knob, an air intake vent, an air output vent, and an electrical connection.

Skills in cooking
Quick Air Crisp Technology and very little oil are used for air-fry meals.
Bake & Roast: The Bake and Roast function enables the appliance to bake and roast a variety of meals, including meat, seafood, and vegetables.
The PowerXL Air Fryer Pro can be used as a slow cooker, particularly for soups, stews, chilis, and other similar dishes.
Your dinner can be entirely cooked using steam.
Meals can be fully and softly grilled using this method.
With this choice, your supper can be fried in a really short period.
This feature maintains the temperature of your meal within acceptable ranges.
The main uses of the PowerXL Air Fryer also include sautéing, simmering, and sous vide cooking.

SNACKS & APPETIZERS RECIPES

Paprika Bacon Shrimp

PREPARATION TIME REQUIRED

Coking Time:	45 minutes
Servings:	10

INGREDIENTS TO USE

1/2 teaspoons red pepper flakes, crushed 1 ¼ pounds shrimp, peeled and deveined
1 tablespoon salt
1 teaspoon paprika
1/2 teaspoon ground black pepper
1 teaspoon chili powder
1 tablespoon shallot powder 1/4 teaspoon cumin powder
¼ pounds thin bacon slices

GOOD STEP BY STEP DIRECTIONS

1. Mix the shrimp with all the spices until they are well-covered.
2. Next, wrap each shrimp in a slice of bacon and secure it with a toothpick. Do this with the rest of the ingredients and let them chill for 30 minutes.
3. Air-fry them in batches at 0 degrees F for 7 to 8 minutes. If you want, serve it with cocktail sticks. Enjoy!

Broccoli Cheese Nuggets

PREPARATION TIME REQUIRED

Coking Time:	15 minutes
Servings:	4

INGREDIENTS TO USE

1/4 cup almond flour
cup broccoli florets, cooked until soft

1 cup cheddar cheese, shredded
egg whites
1/8 tsp salt

GOOD STEP BY STEP DIRECTIONS

1. Set the air fryer's temperature to 325 F.
2. Spray cooking spray in the air fryer basket.
3. Put the cooked broccoli in the bowl and mash it with a fork into small pieces.
4. Then, blend everything in the bowl by adding the remaining ingredients.
5. From the broccoli mixture, form little nuggets and put them in the air fryer basket.
6. For 15 minutes, cook the broccoli nuggets. Midway through, turn.
7. Enjoy after serving.

Mixed Nuts

PREPARATION TIME REQUIRED	
Coking Time:	15 minutes
Servings:	8

INGREDIENTS TO USE

1 tsp. salt
1 tbsp. butter melted 1 tsp. pepper
cup mixed nuts
1 tsp. chipotle chili powder 1 tsp. ground cumin

GOOD STEP BY STEP DIRECTIONS

1. Air Fryer should be heated for five minutes at 350°F.
2. Combine all the ingredients in a bowl, thoroughly coating the nuts.
3. In your fryer basket, add the mixed nuts and roast for 4 minutes, shaking the basket halfway through.

Herb-Roasted Cauliflower

PREPARATION TIME REQUIRED	
Coking Time:	20 minutes
Servings:	2

INGREDIENTS TO USE

4 cups cauliflower florets 2 tablespoons sesame oil
Sea salt and cracked black pepper, to taste
1 teaspoon paprika
1 teaspoon thyme
1 teaspoon sage
1 teaspoon onion powder, 1 teaspoon garlic powder
1 teaspoon rosemary

GOOD STEP BY STEP DIRECTIONS

1. Start by preheating your Air Fryer to 400 degrees F.
2. Toss the cauliflower with the remaining ingredients; toss to coat well.
3. Cook for 12 minutes, shaking the cooking basket halfway through the cooking

time. They will crisp up as they cool. Bon appétit!

Healthy Broccoli Tots

PREPARATION TIME REQUIRED	
Coking Time:	25 minutes
Servings:	4

INGREDIENTS TO USE

1 tsp salt
1/2 cup almond flour
1 lb broccoli, chopped
1/2 tsp garlic powder
1/4 cup ground flaxseed

GOOD STEP BY STEP DIRECTIONS

1. In a microwave-safe bowl, add the broccoli and cook for three minutes.
2. Steamed broccoli should be added to the food processor and processed until it resembles rice.
3. Insert the broccoli into a sizable mixing basin.
4. The other ingredients should be added to the bowl and thoroughly mixed.
5. Spray cooking spray in the air fryer basket.
6. From the broccoli mixture, form little tots and put them in the air fryer basket.
7. At 3 F, cook broccoli tots for 12 minutes.
8. Enjoy after serving.

Baked Cheese Crisps

PREPARATION TIME REQUIRED	
Coking Time:	15 minutes
Servings:	4

INGREDIENTS TO USE

1/2 cup marinara sauce
1 teaspoon Italian seasoning
1/2 cup Parmesan cheese, shredded
1 cup Cheddar cheese, shredded

GOOD STEP BY STEP DIRECTIONS

1. Start by preheating your Air Fryer to 350 degrees F. Place a piece of parchment paper in the cooking basket.
2. Mix the cheese with the Italian seasoning.
3. Add about 1 tablespoon of the cheese mixture (per crisp) to the basket, making sure they are not touching. Bake for 6 minutes or until browned to your liking.
4. Work in batches and place them on a large tray to cool slightly. Serve with marinara sauce. Bon appétit!

Cashew Bowls

PREPARATION TIME REQUIRED	
Coking Time:	5 minutes
Servings:	4

1 teaspoon ranch seasoning
 4 oz cashew
1 teaspoon sesame oil

GOOD STEP BY STEP DIRECTIONS

Set the air fryer to 375F for frying.
Cashews are combined with ranch seasoning and sesame oil and then placed in a preheated air fryer.
For four minutes, cook the cashews.
After a good shake, heat for an additional minute.

Baked Tortillas

Coking Time:	30 minutes
Servings:	4

INGREDIENTS TO USE

Large heads of cauliflower divided into florets
½ tsp salt
Garlic cloves (minced)
1 ½ tsp herbs (whatever your favorite is - basil, oregano, thyme)
4 large eggs

GOOD STEP BY STEP DIRECTIONS

1. your fryer to 375°F/0°C for preheating.
2. Prepare two baking pans with parchment paper.
3. Rice-like cauliflower pieces should be created in a food processor.
4. Riced cauliflower and 1/4 cup water should be added to a pot.
5. Cook for 10 minutes on a medium-high heat until tender. Drain.
6. Use a fresh kitchen towel to dry.

7. Cauliflower, eggs, garlic, herbs, and salt should be combined.
8. On the parchment paper, draw 4 little circles.
9. 20 minutes in the oven, or until dry

Lemon Green Beans

Coking Time:	20 minutes
Servings:	4

INGREDIENTS TO USE

¼ tsp.
Black pepper to taste
1 lemon, juiced
1 lb. green beans, washed and destemmed
extra virgin olive oil sea salt to taste
Directions:

Pre-heat the Air Fryer to 400°F.
Put the green beans in your Air Fryer basket and drizzle the lemon juice over them.
Sprinkle on the pepper and salt. Pour in the oil and toss to coat the green beans well.
Cook for 10 – 12 minutes and serve warm.

Park Rinds

Coking Time:	10 minutes
Servings:	3

INGREDIENTS TO USE

1 teaspoon olive oil
1 tablespoon keto tomato sauce
 6 oz pork skin

GOOD STEP BY STEP DIRECTIONS

Slice the pig skin into rinds, then top with the sauce and oil. Together nicely.
The air fryer should now be heated to 400F.
Cook the pig skin rinds in the air fryer basket for minutes in a single layer.
After frying the rinds for 5 minutes, turn them over.

Kid-Friendly Cocktail Meatballs

PREPARATION TIME REQUIRED	
Coking Time:	20 minutes
Servings:	8

INGREDIENTS TO USE

½ teaspoon fine sea salt
1 cup Romano cheese, grated 3 cloves garlic, minced
½ cup scallions, finely chopped 2 eggs,
well whisked
1/3 teaspoon cumin powder
1½ pound ground pork
2 teaspoons basil
2/3 teaspoon ground black pepper, or more to taste

GOOD STEP BY STEP DIRECTIONS

1. Just stir everything together in a sizable mixing bowl.
2. The meatballs should be formed into bite-sized balls and cooked in an air fryer for 18 minutes at 345 degrees F.
3. If preferred, serve with a zesty sauce, such as marinara. Good appetite!

Spinach Rolls

PREPARATION TIME REQUIRED	
Coking Time:	4 minutes
Servings:	6

INGREDIENTS TO USE

1 cup fresh mint leaves, chopped 1 egg
1 cup fresh parsley, chopped
1 (16-ounces) package of frozen spinach,
thawed 1 red onion, chopped

¼ teaspoon ground cardamom
½ cup Romano cheese, grated
cup of feta cheese, crumbled
tablespoons olive oil
Salt and freshly ground black pepper, as needed 1 package frozen filo dough, thawed

GOOD STEP BY STEP DIRECTIONS

1. In a food processor, combine all the ingredients specified (apart from the oil and filo dough) and process until smooth.
2. On a cutting board, place one filo sheet. Cut into three rectangular strips.
3. Apply oil with a brush to each strip.
4. Add the short side of a strip and about one spoonful of the spinach mixture.
5. To keep the filling in place, roll the dough.
6. Use the remaining filo sheets and spinach mixture in the same manner.
7. Set the Air Fryer to 355 degrees Fahrenheit. Make an Air Fryer basket greased.
8. Rolls should be arranged in a single layer in the prepared basket.
9. For around 4 minutes, air fry.
10. Enjoy!

Cheesy Eggplant Crisps

PREPARATION TIME REQUIRED	
Coking Time:	45 minutes
Servings:	4

INGREDIENTS TO USE

1 teaspoon garlic powder
1/2 teaspoon dried dill weed
1 eggplant, peeled and thinly sliced Salt
1/2 cup almond meal
1/4 cup canola oil
1/2 cup water
1/2 teaspoon ground black pepper, to taste

GOOD STEP BY STEP DIRECTIONS

1. Slices of salted eggplant should be left for around 30 minutes. Slices of eggplant should be squeezed before being rinsed with cold water.
2. Combine the other ingredients and toss in the eggplant segments. Working in batches, cook for 13 minutes at 390 degrees F.
3. Serve with a dipping sauce. Good appetite!

Veggie Sandwich

PREPARATION TIME REQUIRED	
Coking Time:	25 minutes
Servings:	2

INGREDIENTS TO USE

½ cup water
½ tablespoon sugar
¼ of onion, chopped
4 bread slices, trimmed and cut horizontally
For Barbecue Sauce: 1 teaspoon of olive oil
garlic clove, minced
1½ tablespoons tomato ketchup
Salt and ground black pepper, as needed For Sandwich:
tablespoons butter softened 1 cup sweet corn kernels
½ tablespoon Worcestershire sauce
¼ teaspoon mustard powder
1 roasted green bell pepper, chopped

GOOD STEP BY STEP DIRECTIONS

1. For the barbecue sauce, heat the oil in a medium skillet over medium heat and sauté the onion and garlic for about 3–5 minutes.
2. Over high heat, stir in the other ingredients and bring to a boil.
3. Simmer for about 8 to 10 minutes, or until the desired thickness, on medium heat.
4. For the sandwich, heat the butter in a skillet over medium heat while stirring the corn for one to two minutes.
5. Combine the bell pepper, corn, and barbecue sauce in a bowl.
6. Two slices of bread are spread with the corn mixture on one side.
7. Add the remaining slices on top.
8. Set the Air Fryer to 355 degrees Fahrenheit.

9. Put the sandwiches in a single layer in an Air Fryer basket.
10. For around 5 to 6 minutes, air fry.
11. Serve.

Southern Cheese Straws

PREPARATION TIME REQUIRED	
Coking Time:	30 minutes
Servings:	6

INGREDIENTS TO USE

4 ounces of mature Cheddar
cold, freshly grated 1 sticks butter
1 cup all-purpose flour
Sea salt and ground black pepper, to taste
1/2 teaspoon celery seeds
1/4 teaspoon smoked paprika

GOOD STEP BY STEP DIRECTIONS

1. To begin, preheat your air fryer to 330 degrees Fahrenheit.
2. With parchment paper, line the Air Fryer basket.
3. Combine the flour, celery seeds, paprika, salt, and black pepper in a mixing bowl.
4. Then, put the cheese and butter in the stand mixer's bowl. Add the flour mixture slowly while stirring, then thoroughly blend.
5. The dough should then be stuffed into a cookie press with a star disk attached.
6. On the parchment paper, pipe the long dough ribbons in various patterns. After that, cut the lengths into six.
7. For one minute, bake in the preheated Air Fryer.
8. With the remaining dough, repeat. On a rack, let the cheese straws cool. You can keep them in an airtight jar sandwiched between sheets of parchment. Good appetite!

Sage Radish Chips

PREPARATION TIME REQUIRED	
Coking Time:	35 minutes
Servings:	6

INGREDIENTS TO USE

teaspoons avocado oil
½ teaspoon salt
½ teaspoon sage
2 cups radish, sliced

GOOD STEP BY STEP DIRECTIONS

1. Combine the radish, sage, avocado oil, and salt in a mixing basin. the air fryer to 320F for preheating. The sliced radish should be cooked for 35 minutes in the air fryer basket. Every minute, give the vegetables a shake.

Zucchini Rolls

PREPARATION TIME REQUIRED	
Coking Time:	15 minutes
Servings:	2 – 4

INGREDIENTS TO USE

cup goat cheese
1 tbsp. olive oil
¼ tsp. black pepper
zucchini,
sliced thinly lengthwise with a mandolin or a very sharp knife

GOOD STEP BY STEP DIRECTIONS

2. Set your Air Fryer to 390°F for frying.
3. Each zucchini strip should have a thin layer of olive oil applied to it.
4. Goat cheese, black pepper, and sea salt should be combined.
5. Place a small, equal quantity of goat cheese in the middle of each zucchini strip.
6. The strips are rolled up and fastened with toothpicks.
7. Transfer to the Air Fryer and heat the cheese and slightly crisp the zucchini for

minutes. Add additional tomato sauce on top, if desired.

Easy Carrot Dip

PREPARATION TIME REQUIRED	
Coking Time:	15 minutes
Servings:	06-Jan

INGREDIENTS TO USE

1 tbsp chives, chopped Pepper
cups carrots
grated 1/4 tsp cayenne pepper
Salt
4 tbsp butter, melted

GOOD STEP BY STEP DIRECTIONS

1. All ingredients should be added to the baking dish for the air fryer and thoroughly mixed.
2. Cook the dish in the air fryer for 15 minutes at 380 F.
3. Blend the cooked carrot mixture in the blender until it is completely smooth.
4. Enjoy after serving.

Turmeric Cauliflower Popcorn

PREPARATION TIME REQUIRED	
Coking Time:	11 minutes
Servings:	4

INGREDIENTS TO USE

2 tablespoons almond flour 1 teaspoon salt
eggs, beaten
teaspoon ground turmeric
Cooking spray
1 cup cauliflower florets

GOOD STEP BY STEP DIRECTIONS

1.　Smallen the cauliflower florets, then season with salt and crushed turmeric. Then, coat the vegetables with almond flour after dipping them in the eggs.
2.　Set the air fryer to 400F for frying. Cook the cauliflower popcorn in the air fryer for 7 minutes in a single layer. The vegetables should receive a good shake before cooking for an additional 4 minutes.

Sweet Potato Tots

PREPARATION TIME REQUIRED

Coking Time:	31 minutes
Servings:	24

INGREDIENTS TO USE

peeled 1/2 tsp Cajun seasoning Salt
2 sweet potatoes

GOOD STEP BY STEP DIRECTIONS

1.　Bring water to a boil in a big pot by adding it. Add sweet potatoes to the pot and bring to a boil. Good drainage Boiling sweet potatoes shaded into a big bowl.
2.　Sweet potatoes should be finely shredded before adding salt and Cajun seasoning.
3.　Spray cooking spray in the air fryer basket.
4.　Create a little sweet potato tot and place it in the air fryer basket.
5.　Cook for 8 minutes at 400 F. Cook the tots for an additional 8 minutes on the opposite side.
6.　Enjoy after serving.

Cajun Spiced Snack

PREPARATION TIME REQUIRED	
Coking Time:	30 minutes
Servings:	5

INGREDIENTS TO USE

2 tbsp. Cajun or Creole seasoning

½ cup butter, melted 2 cups peanut

2 cups mini wheat thin crackers 2 cups mini pretzels

2 tsp. salt

1 tsp. cayenne pepper 4 cups plain popcorn

1 tsp. paprika

1 tsp. garlic

½ tsp. thyme

½ tsp. oregano

1 tsp. black pepper

½ tsp. onion powder

GOOD STEP BY STEP DIRECTIONS

1. the Air Fryer to a preheated 370°F.
2. Melted butter and Cajun seasoning should be combined in a basin.
3. Combine the peanuts, crackers, popcorn, and pretzels in a separate bowl. Apply the butter mixture to the nibbles.
4. Place in the fryer and cook for 8 to 10 minutes while periodically shaking the basket. This stage must be finished in two groups.
5. Lay the snack mixture out on a baking sheet to cool.
6. For up to a week, the snacks can be stored in an airtight container.

Bacon-wrapped Cheese Croquettes

PREPARATION TIME REQUIRED	
Coking Time:	8 minutes
Servings:	6

INGREDIENTS TO USE

1cup all-purpose flour 3 eggs, 1 cup breadcrumbs

1 tablespoon olive oil Salt, to taste
1-pound thin bacon slices
1-pound sharp cheddar cheese block
cut into 1-inch rectangular pieces

GOOD STEP BY STEP DIRECTIONS

1. Grease an air fryer basket and preheat the air fryer to 390 degrees Fahrenheit.
2. Bacon slices should be completed around one slice of cheddar cheese.
3. Repeat with the rest of the bacon and cheese slices.
4. The croquettes should be placed in a baking dish and frozen for about ten minutes.
5. Put flour in a small bowl. The eggs are beaten in a separate bowl.
6. In a third shallow dish, combine salt, oil, and breadcrumbs.
7. Dip the croquettes in the eggs after uniformly coating them in flour.
8. Place the croquettes in an Air Fryer basket after dredging them in the breadcrumb mixture.
9. Cook for approximately 8 minutes before serving warm.

Mexican Zucchini and Bacon Cakes Ole

PREPARATION TIME REQUIRED	
Coking Time:	22 minutes
Servings:	4

INGREDIENTS TO USE

1/3 teaspoon baking powder, 1/3 cup Swiss cheese
grated 1/3 teaspoons fine sea salt
cup bacon, chopped 1/4 cup almond meal, 1/4 cup coconut flour
small eggs, lightly beaten 1 cup Cotija cheese, grated
1/2 tablespoons fresh basil, finely chopped 1 zucchini, trimmed and grated
1/2 teaspoon freshly cracked black pepper 1 teaspoon Mexican oregano
1/3 cup scallions, finely chopped

GOOD STEP BY STEP DIRECTIONS

1. All ingredients—aside from the Cotija cheese—should be thoroughly mixed.
2. Then, gently press each ball down. Spray nonstick cooking oil on the cakes.
3. Work in batches while you make your cakes for one minute at 305 degrees F.

4.   Serve heatedly with mayonnaise and tomato ketchup.

Mozzarella Sticks

PREPARATION TIME REQUIRED	
Coking Time:	**60 minutes**
Servings:	**4**

INGREDIENTS TO USE

½ oz. pork rinds finely ground
½ cup parmesan cheese
6 x 1-oz. mozzarella string cheese sticks 1 tsp.
dried parsley, grated 2 eggs

GOOD STEP BY STEP DIRECTIONS

The mozzarella sticks should be cut in half and frozen for 45 minutes.

To avoid freezer, burn, you can keep them out for a little while longer and put them in a Ziploc bag.

Pork rinds, parmesan cheese, and dried parsley should all be combined in a small basin.

Fork-beat the eggs in a different bowl.

Frozen mozzarella sticks should be coated completely after being dipped into the eggs and the mixture of pig rinds. Place the remaining cheese sticks in the basket of your air fryer after coating each one. Cook for 10 minutes, or until golden brown, at 400°F.

Serve hot, and if preferred, top with some homemade marinara sauce.

Simple Banana Chips

PREPARATION TIME REQUIRED	
Coking Time:	10 minutes
Servings:	8

INGREDIENTS TO USE

2 raw bananas, peeled and sliced 2 tablespoons olive oil, Salt, and black pepper, to taste

GOOD STEP BY STEP DIRECTIONS

Grease the air fryer basket and preheat the air fryer to 355 degrees Fahrenheit.
Place banana slices in the Air Fryer basket and equally drizzle with olive oil.
After about 10 minutes of cooking, add salt and black pepper to taste.
Serve the prepared food warmly.

Brussels Sprouts With Feta Cheese

PREPARATION TIME REQUIRED	
Coking Time:	20 minutes
Servings:	4

INGREDIENTS TO USE

3/4-pound Brussels sprouts
trimmed and cut off the ends with 1 teaspoon kosher salt
1 tablespoon lemon zest non-stick cooking spray, cup feta cheese, cubed

GOOD STEP BY STEP DIRECTIONS

1. The Brussels sprouts should first be peeled using a tiny paring knife. Toss the leaves with salt and lemon zest before spraying all sides with cooking spray.
2. After 8 minutes of baking at 380 degrees, shake the frying basket and continue baking for another 7 minutes. Work in batches to ensure even cooking of all the food. Adjust the seasonings based on taste.
3. Add feta cheese to the dish. Good appetite!

Cumin Pork Sticks

PREPARATION TIME REQUIRED	
Coking Time:	12 minutes
Servings:	4

INGREDIENTS TO USE

¼ teaspoon ground cumin 8 oz pork loin

1 teaspoon sunflower oil

½ teaspoon chili powder

Eggs, beaten

4 tablespoons flax meal

GOOD STEP BY STEP DIRECTIONS

1. Slice the pork loin into sticks and season with cumin and chili powder. Then, cover the pork sticks with a flax meal after dipping them in the eggs.
2. Spray sunflower oil on the meat before placing it in the air fryer. Cook the snack for 6 minutes at 400F.
3. then turn
4. Cook the pork sticks for an additional 6 minutes on the opposite side.

Bell Pepper Chips

PREPARATION TIME REQUIRED	
Coking Time:	**20 minutes**
Servings:	**4**

INGREDIENTS TO USE

3/4-pound bell peppers, deveined and cut to 1/4-inch strips
2 tablespoons grapeseed oil
1/2 cup parmesan, grated with 1 teaspoon sea salt
1/2 teaspoons red pepper flakes, crushed, 1 egg, beaten

GOOD STEP BY STEP DIRECTIONS

The egg, parmesan, salt, and red pepper flakes should all be combined thoroughly in a mixing dish.

Bell peppers are placed in the cooking basket after being dipped in the batter. Use grapeseed oil to brush.

Cook for 4 minutes at 0 degrees F in the air fryer that has been preheated. Cook for an additional three minutes after shaking the basket. Work in groups.

After tasting, season as needed, and serving. Good appetite!

Crunchy Bacon Bites

PREPARATION TIME REQUIRED	
Coking Time:	**10 minutes**
Servings:	**4**

INGREDIENTS TO USE

1/4 cup hot sauce
4 bacon strips, cut into small pieces 1/2 cup pork rinds, crushed

GOOD STEP BY STEP DIRECTIONS

1. Add some bacon to the bowl. Stir thoroughly after adding the spicy sauce.
2. Once the bacon bits are thoroughly coated, add the crumbled pig rinds and stir.
3. Place the bacon slices in the air fryer basket and cook for 10 minutes at 350 F.
4. Enjoy after serving.

Broccoli Fries with Spicy Dip

PREPARATION TIME REQUIRED	
Coking Time:	15 minutes
Servings:	4

INGREDIENTS TO USE

1/4 cup mayonnaise 1/4 cup Greek yogurt
1/4 teaspoon Dijon mustard 1 teaspoon hot sauce
4 tablespoons parmesan cheese, preferably freshly grated Spicy Dip:
3/4-pound broccoli florets 1/2 teaspoon onion powder
Sea salt and ground black pepper, to taste 2 tablespoons sesame oil
1 teaspoon granulated garlic 1/2 teaspoon cayenne pepper

GOOD STEP BY STEP DIRECTIONS

1. Add some bacon to the bowl. Stir thoroughly after adding the spicy sauce.
2. Once the bacon bits are thoroughly coated, add the crumbled pig rinds and stir.
3. Place the bacon slices in the air fryer basket and cook for 10 minutes at 350 F.
4. Enjoy after serving.

Spicy Dip

PREPARATION TIME REQUIRED	
Coking Time:	5 minutes
Servings:	6

INGREDIENTS TO USE

1 1/2 cups apple cider vinegar pepper
Salt
12 oz hot peppers, chopped

GOOD STEP BY STEP DIRECTIONS

1. Stir everything together before adding it to the baking dish for the air fryer.
2. Cook the meal in the air fryer for 5 minutes at 380 F.
3. Blend the pepper mixture in the blender until it is completely smooth.
4. Enjoy after serving.

Crunchy Broccoli Fries

PREPARATION TIME REQUIRED	
Coking Time:	15 minutes
Servings:	4

INGREDIENTS TO USE

Sea salt and ground black pepper, to taste 2 tablespoons sesame oil

4 tablespoons parmesan cheese, preferably freshly grated

1/2 teaspoon cayenne pepper

1 pound broccoli florets

1/2 teaspoon onion powder 1 teaspoon granulated garlic

GOOD STEP BY STEP DIRECTIONS

1. Stir everything together before adding it to the baking dish for the air fryer.
2. Cook the meal in the air fryer for 5 minutes at 380 F.
3. Blend the pepper mixture in the blender until it is completely smooth.
4. Enjoy after serving.

Cheesy Zucchini Sticks

PREPARATION TIME REQUIRED	
Coking Time:	20 minutes
Servings:	2

INGREDIENTS TO USE

Sea salt and black pepper,
to your liking 1 tablespoon garlic powder
1/2 teaspoon red pepper flakes
1/4 cup Romano cheese, shredded
1 zucchini, sliced into strips 2 tablespoons mayonnaise
1/4 cup tortilla chips, crushed

GOOD STEP BY STEP DIRECTIONS

1. Apply mayonnaise on the zucchini.
2. In a shallow bowl, combine the cheese, crushed tortilla chips, and seasonings.
3. Then, sprinkle the cheese/chips mixture over the zucchini sticks.
4. Cook for 12 minutes at 0 degrees F in the preheated Air Fryer while shaking the basket halfway through.
5. Work in batches to get the sticks golden brown and crispy. Good appetite!

BBQ Lil Smokies

PREPARATION TIME REQUIRED	
Coking Time:	20 minutes
Servings:	6

INGREDIENTS TO USE

1 pound beef cocktail wieners
10 ounces barbecue sauce, no sugar added

GOOD STEP BY STEP DIRECTIONS

1. To begin with, preheat your air fryer to 380 degrees Fahrenheit.
2. Put your sausages on the baking sheet after using a fork to prick holes into them.
3. For one minute, cook.

4.   Give the pan another two minutes of cooking after adding the barbecue sauce.
5.   Use toothpicks to eat.
6.   Good appetite!

Baby Corn

PREPARATION TIME REQUIRED	
Coking Time:	**20 minutes**
Servings:	**4**

INGREDIENTS TO USE

½ tsp. carom seeds
8 oz. baby corn, boiled 1 cup flour
¼ tsp. chili powder Pinch of baking soda Salt to taste
1 tsp. Garlic powder

GOOD STEP BY STEP DIRECTIONS

1. Combine the flour, carom seed, cooking soda, salt, cayenne pepper, chili powder, and garlic powder in a bowl. To achieve the consistency of the batter, add a little water.
2. Each tiny corn should be batter-coated. Set the Air Fryer to 0°F for heating.
3. Lay the coated baby corn on top of the aluminum foil covering the Air Fryer basket.
4. For 10 minutes, cook.

Summer Meatball Skewers

PREPARATION TIME REQUIRED	
Coking Time:	**20 minutes**
Servings:	**6**

INGREDIENTS TO USE

red pepper,
1-inch piece 1 cup pearl onions
1/2 cup barbecue sauce
1 teaspoon fresh garlic,
minced 1 teaspoon dried parsley flakes Salt and black pepper, to taste
1/2-pound ground pork 1/2-pound ground beef
1 teaspoon dried onion flakes

GOOD STEP BY STEP DIRECTIONS

1. Onion flakes, garlic flakes, parsley flakes, salt, and black pepper should all be combined with ground beef. Using the mixture, form inch-sized balls.
2. Alternately thread meatballs, peppers, and pearl onions onto skewers.
3. The barbecue sauce should be heated for 10 seconds.
4. Cook for 5 minutes at 380 degrees in the prepared Air Fryer. About halfway through the cooking process, flip the skewers over. After adding the sauce, simmer for an additional 5 minutes. Work in groups.
5. Enjoy serving with the remaining barbecue sauce!

Cauliflower Bombs with Sweet & Sour Sauce

PREPARATION TIME REQUIRED	
Coking Time:	25 minutes
Servings:	4

INGREDIENTS TO USE

jarred 1 clove garlic, minced

ounces Ricotta cheese 1/3 cup Swiss cheese

Salt and black pepper, to taste

1 egg

1 tablespoon Italian seasoning mix Sweet & Sour Sauce:

1 red bell pepper,

1 teaspoon sherry vinegar 1 tablespoon tomato puree 2 tablespoons olive oil

Cauliflower Bombs: 1/2-pound cauliflower

GOOD STEP BY STEP DIRECTIONS

1. Cook the cauliflower for 3 to 4 minutes, or until it is al dente, in salted boiling water. Once thoroughly drained, pulse in a food processor.
2. Add and thoroughly combine the remaining ingredients for the cauliflower bombs.
3. For 16 minutes, bake at 5 degrees F in the preheated Air Fryer while shaking the pan halfway through.
4. While waiting, blend all of the sauce's components in your food processor. according to taste. Cauliflower bombs should be served with Sweet & Sour Sauce on the side. Good appetite!

Fried Pickle Chips with Greek Yogurt Dip

PREPARATION TIME REQUIRED

Coking Time:	**20 minutes**
Servings:	**5**

INGREDIENTS TO USE

Cup pickle chips, pat dry with kitchen towels Greek Yogurt Dip:

1/2 cup Greek yogurt 1 clove garlic, minced

1/2 cup cornmeal

1/4 teaspoon ground black pepper 1 tablespoon fresh chives, chopped

1/2 cup all-purpose flour

teaspoon cayenne pepper 1/2 teaspoon shallot powder 1 teaspoon garlic powder 1/2 teaspoon porcini powder

Kosher salt and ground black pepper, to taste 2 eggs

GOOD STEP BY STEP DIRECTIONS

1. Mix the cornmeal and flour in a small basin. Add the seasonings and stir to thoroughly blend. In a separate shallow bowl, beat the eggs.
2. Pickle chips should be dredged in the flour mixture first, followed by the egg mixture. Pickle chips are evenly coated after being pressed into the flour mixture once more.
3. Shake the basket and cook for a further 5 minutes in the preheated Air Fryer at 400 degrees F. Work in groups.
4. In the meantime, thoroughly blend all the sauce components. Enjoy the Greek yogurt dip with the fried pickles.

Old-fashioned Onion Rings

PREPARATION TIME REQUIRED	
Coking Time:	10 minutes
Servings:	4

INGREDIENTS TO USE

¾ cup dry bread crumbs Salt, to taste
egg
1 large onion, cut into rings 1¼ cups all-purpose flour
1 cup milk

GOOD STEP BY STEP DIRECTIONS

1. Grease the Air Fryer basket and preheat the Air Fryer to 360°F.
2. Salt and flour should be combined on a plate.
3. In a separate bowl, combine the egg and milk thoroughly. In a third dish, add the breadcrumbs.
4. After dipping the onion rings in the egg mixture, coat them with the flour mixture.
5. The onion rings are then placed in the air fryer basket after being coated in breadcrumbs.
6. After about 10 minutes, remove the food and serve it warm.

Cashew Dip

PREPARATION TIME REQUIRED	
Coking Time:	8 minutes
Servings:	6

INGREDIENTS TO USE

A pinch of salt and black pepper, 2 tablespoons coconut milk
garlic cloves, minced 1 teaspoon lime juice
½ cup cashews, soaked in water for 4 hours
and drained 3 tablespoons cilantro, chopped

GOOD STEP BY STEP DIRECTIONS

1. Blend all the ingredients in a blender, then pour into a ramekin. The ramekin should be placed in the basket of your air fryer and cooked for 8 minutes at 350 degrees F. Use it as a dip for a party.

Sweet Potato Bites

PREPARATION TIME REQUIRED	
Coking Time:	30 minutes
Servings:	2

INGREDIENTS TO USE

2 tsp. cinnamon 2 tbsp. olive oil 2 tbsp. honey
2 sweet potatoes, diced into 1-inch cubes 1 tsp. red chili flakes
½ cup fresh parsley, chopped

GOOD STEP BY STEP DIRECTIONS

1. the Air Fryer to 350°F before use.
2. To completely coat the sweet potato cubes, combine all the ingredients in a bowl and whisk thoroughly.
3. Cook the sweet potato combination for 15 minutes in the Air Fryer basket.

Roasted Peanuts

PREPARATION TIME REQUIRED	
Coking Time:	14 minutes
Servings:	10

2½ cups raw peanuts 1 tablespoon olive oil Salt, as required

GOOD STEP BY STEP DIRECTIONS

1. Set the Air Fryer to 320 degrees Fahrenheit.
2. Place the peanuts in a single layer in an Air Fryer basket.
3. Tossing twice, air fry for around 9 minutes.
4. The peanuts should be taken out of the Air Fryer basket and placed in a basin.
5. Add the salt and oil, then toss to evenly coat.
6. the nut mixture back into the Air Fryer basket.
7. For around five minutes, air fry.
8. Put the hot nuts in a glass or steel dish once you're finished, then serve.

Crispy Eggplant

PREPARATION TIME REQUIRED	
Coking Time:	20 minutes
Servings:	4

INGREDIENTS TO USE

1/2 tsp Italian seasoning 1 tsp paprika
1 eggplant, cut into 1-inch pieces
1/2 tsp red pepper 1 tsp garlic powder 2 tbsp olive oil

GOOD STEP BY STEP DIRECTIONS

1. Toss everything together in a big mixing bowl after adding it.
2. Insert the basket of the air fryer with the eggplant mixture.
3. Cook for 20 minutes at 5 F. halfway through, shaking the basket.
4. Enjoy after serving.

Party Chicken Pillows

PREPARATION TIME REQUIRED	
Coking Time:	20 minutes
Servings:	4

INGREDIENTS TO USE

4 tablespoons tomato paste

4 ounces of cream cheese, at room temperature

2 tablespoons butter, melted

1 teaspoon olive oil

1 teaspoon onion powder and 1/2 teaspoon garlic powder

1 cup ground chicken

1 (8-ounces) can Pillsbury Crescent Roll dough sea salt and ground black pepper, to taste

GOOD STEP BY STEP DIRECTIONS

1. In a pan, heat the olive oil to a medium-high temperature. Then, sauté the ground chicken for 4 minutes, or until it is browned.
2. The dough crescent is unrolled. Cut the dough into 8 pieces after flattening it out with a rolling pin.
3. In the middle of each piece, add the cheese, tomato paste, onion, garlic, salt, and black pepper-browned chicken.
4. Using wet hands, fold each corner over the filling. Edges should be sealed after pressing together to completely cover the filling.
5. Spray some cooking oil on the Air Fryer basket's base now. In the cooking basket, arrange the chicken pillows in a single layer. Sprinkle the chicken pillows with melted butter.
6. Bake for minutes at 370 degrees F, or until golden brown. Work in groups. Good appetite!

Vegetable Mix

PREPARATION TIME REQUIRED	
Coking Time:	45 minutes
Servings:	4

INGREDIENTS TO USE

Epaulet pepper to taste 1 tbsp. Olive oil

3.5 oz. pumpkin

3.5 oz. Parsnips Salt to taste

4 cloves garlic, unpeeled

3.5 oz. celeriac 1 yellow carrot 1 orange carrot 1 red onion

3.5 oz. radish

½ tsp. Parsley

GOOD STEP BY STEP DIRECTIONS

1. All the vegetables should be peeled and cut into 2- to 3-cm pieces.
2. Set your Air Fryer to 390°F before using.
3. The oil should be added and given time to warm up before the vegetables, garlic, salt, and pepper are added to the fryer.
4. For 18 to 20 minutes.
5. If desired, serve hot over rice and garnish with parsley.

Quick and Easy Popcorn

PREPARATION TIME REQUIRED	
Coking Time:	20 minutes
Servings:	4

INGREDIENTS TO USE

1 teaspoon red pepper flakes, crushed

Kosher salt, to taste

2 tablespoons dried corn kernels 1 teaspoon safflower oil

GOOD STEP BY STEP DIRECTIONS

1. Fill the Air Fryer basket with the dried corn kernels and brush with safflower oil.

2. Cook for 15 minutes at 395 degrees F, shaking the basket every five minutes.
3. Salt and red pepper flakes should be added. Good appetite!

Cheese Dill Mushrooms

PREPARATION TIME REQUIRED	
Coking Time:	5 minutes
Servings:	6

INGREDIENTS TO USE

6 oz cheddar cheese, shredded 1 tbsp butter
1/2 tsp salt
1 tsp dried dill
9 oz mushrooms, cut stems 1 tsp dried parsley

GOOD STEP BY STEP DIRECTIONS

1. Finely chop the mushroom stem and add to the bowl.
2. Then, add the parsley, dill, cheese, butter, and salt to the bowl.
3. Turn the air fryer on at 400 F.
4. Place the mushroom caps in the air fryer basket after stuffing them with the bowl mixture.
5. Cook mushrooms for a short while.
6. Enjoy after serving.

Simple Radish Chips

PREPARATION TIME REQUIRED	
Coking Time:	15 minutes
Servings:	12

1/4 tsp pepper

1 tsp salt

lb radish, wash and slice into chips 2 tbsp olive oil

GOOD STEP BY STEP DIRECTIONS

1. Set the air fryer to 375 degrees.
2. Toss everything together in the big bowl after adding it.
3. Slice up some radishes and place them in the air fryer basket. Cook for 15 minutes. While cooking, jiggle the basket twice.
4. Enjoy after serving.

Roasted Parsnip

PREPARATION TIME REQUIRED	
Coking Time:	55 minutes
Servings:	5

1 tbsp. parsley, dried flakes

1 tbsp. Coconut oil

lb. parsnips [about 6 large parsnips] 2 tbsp. Maple syrup

GOOD STEP BY STEP DIRECTIONS

1. In your Air Fryer, melt the coconut oil or duck fat for 2 minutes at 320°F.
2. The parsnips should be rinsed, dried, and cleaned. Cut into cubes of 1 inch. Place it in the fryer.
3. For 35 minutes, stir the parsnip cubes often in the fat/oil.
4. To obtain a soft texture throughout, season the parsnips with parsley and maple syrup and simmer for an additional five minutes or longer. Serve immediately.

Apple Chips

PREPARATION TIME REQUIRED	
Coking Time:	16 minutes
Servings:	2

INGREDIENTS TO USE

Apple, peeled, cored, and thinly sliced 1 tablespoon sugar
½ teaspoon ground cinnamon A pinch of ground cardamom A pinch of ground ginger
A pinch of salt

GOOD STEP BY STEP DIRECTIONS

1. Set the temperature of the Air Fryer to 390 degrees F.
2. In a bowl, add all the ingredients and toss to coat well.
3. Arrange the apple slices in an Air Fryer basket in a single layer in 2 batches.
4. Air Fry for about 7-8 minutes, flipping once halfway through.
5. Serve.

Polenta Sticks

PREPARATION TIME REQUIRED	
Coking Time:	6 minutes
Servings:	4

INGREDIENTS TO USE

2½ cups cooked polenta Salt, as required
¼ cup Parmesan cheese, shredded

GOOD STEP BY STEP DIRECTIONS

1. Add the polenta evenly to a greased baking dish with the back of a spoon, smooth the top surface.
2. Cover the baking dish and refrigerate for about 1 hour or until set.
3. Remove from the refrigerator and cut down the polenta into the desired size slices.
4. Set the temperature of the Air Fryer to 350 degrees F. Grease a baking dish.
5. Arrange the polenta sticks into the prepared baking dish in a single layer and

sprinkle with salt.
6.   Place the baking dish into an Air Fryer basket.
7.   Air Fry for about 5-6 minutes.
8.   Top with the cheese and serve.

Fried Green Tomatoes

PREPARATION TIME REQUIRED	
Coking Time:	10 minutes
Servings:	2

INGREDIENTS TO USE

¼ cup blanched finely ground flour
1/3 cup parmesan cheese, grated
medium green tomatoes 1 egg

GOOD STEP BY STEP DIRECTIONS

1. Slice the tomatoes thinly—about half an inch.
2. Whisk the egg after cracking it into a bowl. Combine the parmesan cheese and flour in a different basin.
3. Egg-dredge the tomato slices before coating them with the flour-cheese mixture. Put a slice of bread in the frying basket. They might require cooking in several batches.
4. Serve them warm after frying them at 0°F for seven minutes, turning them over halfway through.

Coconut Cookies

PREPARATION TIME REQUIRED	
Coking Time:	12 minutes
Servings:	8

INGREDIENTS TO USE

1¼ ounces white chocolate, chopped 3 tablespoons desiccated coconut
1 small egg
2¼ ounces caster sugar 3½ ounces butter
teaspoon vanilla extract 5 ounces of self-rising flour

GOOD STEP BY STEP DIRECTIONS

In a large bowl, add the sugar and butter and beat until fluffy and light.

1. Slice the tomatoes thinly—about half an inch.
2. Whisk the egg after cracking it into a bowl. Combine the parmesan cheese and flour in a different basin.
3. Egg-dredge the tomato slices before coating them with the flour-cheese mixture. Put a slice of bread in the frying basket. They might require cooking in several batches.
4. Serve them warm after frying them at 0°F for seven minutes, turning them over halfway through.

Crust-less Meaty Pizza

PREPARATION TIME REQUIRED	
Coking Time:	1 minutes
Servings:	15

INGREDIENTS TO USE

¼ cup ground sausage, cooked 7 slices pepperoni
Sliced sugar-free bacon, cooked and crumbled
1 tbsp. Parmesan cheese, grated
½ cup mozzarella cheese, shredded

GOOD STEP BY STEP DIRECTIONS

1. Using a six-inch cake pan, cover the bottom with mozzarella. Add the bacon,

sausage, and pepperoni, and then top with a little parmesan cheese.
2.   The pan should be put inside your air fryer.
3.   Cook for five minutes at 400°F. When the cheese is bubbling and brown in color, it is finished.
4.   When taking the pan out of the fryer to serve, be careful.

Spinach Dip

PREPARATION TIME REQUIRED	
Coking Time:	40 minutes
Servings:	8

INGREDIENTS TO USE

drained and chopped 1 cup mayonnaise
1 cup parmesan cheese, grated
1/2 cup onion, minced
1/3 cup water chestnuts
1 cup frozen spinach, thawed and squeezed out all liquid 1/2 tsp pepper
8 oz cream cheese
softened 1/4 tsp garlic powder

GOOD STEP BY STEP DIRECTIONS

1.   Apply cooking spray to the baking pan for the air fryer.
2.   Mix each ingredient thoroughly after adding it to the bowl.
3.   Place baking dish in the air fryer basket after adding the bowl mixture to it.
4.   Cook for 35 minutes at 300 F. Stir in the dip after cooking for 20 minutes.
5.   Enjoy after serving.

Italian-style Tomato-parmesan Crisps

PREPARATION TIME REQUIRED	
Coking Time:	20 minutes
Servings:	4

INGREDIENTS TO USE

Sea salt and white pepper, to taste 1 teaspoon Italian seasoning mix
4 tablespoons Parmesan cheese, grated
2 tablespoons olive oil

4 Roma tomatoes

GOOD STEP BY STEP DIRECTIONS

1. Set your Air Fryer to 350 degrees Fahrenheit to begin. Grease the Air Fryer basket with a generous amount of nonstick cooking oil.
2. Combine the other ingredients and toss in the tomato slices. Without overlapping, transfer them to the frying basket.
3. Cook for 5 minutes in a preheated Air Fryer. Cook for a further five minutes while shaking the cooking basket. Work in groups.
4. If desired, serve with Mediterranean aioli for dipping. Good appetite!

Cocktail Flanks

PREPARATION TIME REQUIRED	
Coking Time:	45 minutes
Servings:	4

can crescent rolls
1x 12-oz. package cocktail franks 1x 8-oz.

GOOD STEP BY STEP DIRECTIONS

1. After draining, use paper towels to dry the cocktail franks.
2. The crescent rolls should now be unrolled, and the dough should be cut into 1" by 1.5" rectangular pieces.
3. With the ends sticking out, wrap the strips around the franks.
4. Place for five minutes in the freezer.
5. the Air Fryer to 330°F before use.
6. Put the franks in the cooking basket after removing them from the freezer.
7. Cook for 6 to 8 minutes.
8. To get a golden-brown color, lower the heat to 390°F and continue cooking for an additional 3 minutes.

Bacon Croquettes

PREPARATION TIME REQUIRED

Coking Time:	8 minutes
Servings:	6

INGREDIENTS TO USE

1 cup breadcrumbs Salt, as required

1 cup all-purpose flour, 3 eggs

¼ cup olive oil

1-pound thin bacon slices

1-pound sharp cheddar cheese block, cut into 1-inch rectangular pieces

GOOD STEP BY STEP DIRECTIONS

1. Two bacon slices should completely encircle a piece of cheddar cheese.
2. Continue with the remaining slices of bacon and cheese.
3. The croquettes should be placed in a baking dish and frozen for around five minutes.
4. Fill the small dish with flour.
5. Crack the eggs and beat them well in a separate bowl.
6. Combine the breadcrumbs, salt, and oil in a third dish.
7. The croquettes should first be covered in flour, then dipped in beaten eggs, and then equally covered with the breadcrumb mixture.
8. Set the Air Fryer to 390 degrees Fahrenheit.
9. Place the croquettes in a single layer in an Air Fryer basket.
10. For 7-8 minutes, air fry.
11. Serve warm.

Cheese Bacon Jalapeno Poppers

PREPARATION TIME REQUIRED	
Coking Time:	5 minutes
Servings:	5

INGREDIENTS TO USE

shredded 6 oz cream cheese, softened
10 fresh jalapeno peppers, cut in half and remove seeds, 2 bacon slices, cooked and crumbled
1/4 cup cheddar cheese

GOOD STEP BY STEP DIRECTIONS

1. Cheddar cheese, bacon, and cream cheese should all be combined in a bowl.
2. Fill the halves of each jalapeño with the bacon cheese mixture.
3. Spray cooking spray in the air fryer basket.
4. Half a stuffed jalapeño should be placed in an air fryer basket and cooked for 5 minutes at 370 F.
5. Enjoy after serving.

Grilled Cheese Sandwiches

PREPARATION TIME REQUIRED	
Coking Time:	5 minutes
Servings:	2

INGREDIENTS TO USE

½ cup sharp cheddar cheese,
1 tablespoon mayonnaise
½ cup melted butter softened
4 white bread slices

GOOD STEP BY STEP DIRECTIONS

1. Grease the air fryer basket and preheat the air fryer to 355 degrees Fahrenheit.
2. Each piece of bread should have mayonnaise and butter spread over one side.
3. On the two slices' buttered sides, scatter the cheddar cheese.
4. Transfer to the Air Fryer basket and top with the remaining slices of bread.
5. Cook for a few minutes before serving warm.

Cheese Pastries

PREPARATION TIME REQUIRED	
Coking Time:	5 minutes
Servings:	6

INGREDIENTS TO USE

2 tablespoons fresh parsley, finely chopped salt, and ground black pepper, as needed
2 frozen filo pastry sheets, thawed 2 tablespoons olive oil
4 ounces feta cheese, crumbled 1 scallion, finely chopped
1 egg yolk

INGREDIENTS TO USE

1. Add the egg yolk to a big basin and beat it vigorously.
2. Feta cheese, scallions, parsley, salt, and black pepper should be added. Mix well.
3. Slice each sheet of filo pastry into three strips.

4. On the bottom of the strip, spread approximately 1 teaspoon of the feta mixture.
5. To create a triangle, zigzag the sheet's tip over the filler.
6. Use leftover strips and fillings to repeat the process.
7. Set the Air Fryer to 390 degrees Fahrenheit.
8. Distribute the oil equally over each pastry.
9. Put the pastries in a single layer in an Air Fryer basket.
10. Air fryer for around 2 minutes at 360 degrees F after about 3 minutes of air frying.
11. Serve.

Pizza Bites

PREPARATION TIME REQUIRED	
Coking Time:	3 minutes
Servings:	10

INGREDIENTS TO USE

10 mozzarella cheese slices and 10 pepperoni slices

GOOD STEP BY STEP DIRECTIONS

1. Set the air fryer to 400F for frying. Spread mozzarella in a single layer on the baking paper-lined air fryer pan. After that, put the pan inside the air fryer basket and melt the cheese there for 3 minutes. The cheese should now be taken out of the air fryer and allowed to cool to room temperature. After that, take the cheese off the parchment paper and top it with the pepperoni pieces. The cheese should be folded into turnovers.

Pineapple Bites with Yogurt Dip

PREPARATION TIME REQUIRED	
Coking Time:	10 minutes
Servings:	4

INGREDIENTS TO USE

1 tablespoon fresh mint leaves, minced 1 green chili, chopped
1 cup vanilla yogurt 1 tablespoon honey
½ of pineapple, cut into long 1-2-inch-thick sticks
¼ cup desiccated coconut

GOOD STEP BY STEP DIRECTIONS

Grease the air fryer basket and preheat the air fryer to 390 degrees Fahrenheit.
The coconut should be put on a small plate.
Sticks of pineapple are dipped in honey and then coated with coconut.
Place the pineapple sticks in the basket of the Air Fryer and cook for approximately 10 minutes.
Yogurt dip:

In a bowl, combine vanilla yogurt, mint, and Chile.
These pineapple sticks should be served with yogurt dip.

Chocolate Bacon Bites

PREPARATION TIME REQUIRED	
Coking Time:	10 minutes
Servings:	4

1 cup dark chocolate, melted A pinch of pink salt
4 bacon slices, halved

GOOD STEP BY STEP DIRECTIONS

1. Each bacon slice should be covered in some chocolate and pink salt before being placed in the basket of your air fryer and heated for several minutes at 350 degrees F. As a snack, give. Each bacon slice should be covered in some chocolate and pink salt before being placed in the basket of your air fryer and heated for several minutes at 350 degrees F. As a snack, give.

Avocado Wedges

PREPARATION TIME REQUIRED	
Coking Time:	8 minutes
Servings:	4

INGREDIENTS TO USE

A pinch of salt and black pepper cooking spray
1 and ½ cups almond meal
4 avocados, peeled, pitted
and cut into wedges 1 egg, whisked

GOOD STEP BY STEP DIRECTIONS

1. Put the almond meal in one bowl and the egg in another. Avocado wedges are salted and peppered before being egg- and meal-almond-crusted. The avocado bites should be arranged in the basket of your air fryer, greased with cooking spray, and cooked for 8 minutes at 400 degrees F.
2. Serve immediately as a snack.

Saucy Asian Short Ribs

PREPARATION TIME REQUIRED	
Coking Time:	35 minutes
Servings:	4

INGREDIENTS TO USE

1 teaspoon kochukaru (chili pepper flakes) Sea salt and ground black pepper, to taste 1 tablespoon sesame oil

1 tablespoon Sriracha sauce 2 garlic cloves, minced

pound meaty short ribs 1/2 rice vinegar

tablespoons soy sauce

1 tablespoon doenjang (soybean paste)

1/4 cup green onions, roughly chopped

GOOD STEP BY STEP DIRECTIONS

1. Short ribs, vinegar, soy sauce, Sriracha, garlic, and spices should all be combined in a Ziploc bag and marinated for the entire night.
2. Sesame oil should be rubbed onto the Air Fryer basket's bottom and sides. Transfer the ribs to the prepared frying basket after discarding the marinade.
3. The marinated ribs should be cooked for 17 minutes at 5 degrees in a preheated Air Fryer. Cook the ribs for an additional 15 minutes on the other side, then brush with the marinade you set aside.
4. Green onions are garnished. Good appetite!

Lemon Tofu

PREPARATION TIME REQUIRED	
Coking Time:	15 minutes
Servings:	4

INGREDIENTS TO USE

1/2 cup water

tbsp tamari for the sauce:

tsp arrowroot powder 2 tbsp erythritol

1/3 cup lemon juice 1 tsp lemon zest

1 lb tofu, drained and pressed with 1 tbsp arrowroot powder

GOOD STEP BY STEP DIRECTIONS

Tofu should be cubed. Shake thoroughly after adding the tofu and tamari to the zip-lock bag.

To coat the tofu, add 1 tablespoon of arrowroot to the bag and shake well. Wait 15 minutes before moving.

In the meantime, combine all sauce ingredients in a bowl and set away.

Spray cooking spray in the air fryer basket.

Tofu should be added to the air fryer basket and cooked for 10 minutes at 390 F. halfway through, shake.

6.

Cook the cooked tofu and sauce mixture in the pan for 3-5 minutes on a medium-high heat.

7.

Enjoy after serving.

Mexican Muffins

PREPARATION TIME REQUIRED	
Coking Time:	15 minutes
Servings:	4

INGREDIENTS TO USE

oz Mexican blended cheese,
Shredded 1 teaspoon keto tomato sauce cooking spray
teaspoon taco seasonings
1 cup ground beef

GOOD STEP BY STEP DIRECTIONS

1. Set the air fryer to 375F for frying. Ground beef and taco seasoning should be combined in the meantime in a mixing dish. Cooking spray should be used on muffin tins. After that, place the ground beef mixture in the muffin tins and top each with a tomato and a slice of cheese.
2. sauce. Place the muffin tins in the air fryer that has been prepared and cook them for a few minutes.

CARROTS & RHUBARB

Party Time Mixed Nuts

PREPARATION TIME REQUIRED	
Coking Time:	14 minutes
Servings:	3

INGREDIENTS TO USE

½ cup raisins

½ cup pecans

1 tablespoon olive oil Salt, to taste

½ cup raw almonds

½ cup raw cashew nuts, ½ cup raw peanuts

GOOD STEP BY STEP DIRECTIONS

1. Grease the air fryer basket and heat the air fryer to 320 degrees Fahrenheit.
2. The nuts should be cooked in the Air Fryer basket for around 9 minutes, tossing twice throughout that time.
3. The nuts should be taken out of the Air Fryer basket and placed in a basin.
4. Sprinkle with salt and olive oil, then toss to evenly coat.
5. Once more, add the nut mixture to the basket of the Air Fryer, and cook for a few minutes.
6. Serve the prepared food warmly.

Curly's Cauliflower

PREPARATION TIME REQUIRED	
Coking Time:	30 minutes
Servings:	4

INGREDIENTS TO USE

¼ cup buffalo sauce [vegan/other]
Cup-friendly bread crumbs, mixed with 1 tsp. salt
4 cups bite-sized cauliflower florets
¼ cup melted butter [vegan/other]
Mayo [vegan/other] or creamy dressing for dipping

GOOD STEP BY STEP DIRECTIONS

1. To make a creamy paste, mix the butter and buffalo sauce in a bowl.
2. Spread the sauce over each floret entirely.
3. Sprinkle the bread crumbs mixture over the florets. The florets should be cooked in the Air Fryer for around 15 minutes at 350°F while occasionally shaking the basket.
4. Serve with a creamy sauce, mayo, or raw veggie salad.

Avocado Fries with Chipotle Sauce

PREPARATION TIME REQUIRED

Coking Time:	20 minutes
Servings:	3

INGREDIENTS TO USE

1/2 cup breadcrumbs

Pink Himalayan salt and ground white pepper, to taste 1/4 cup flour

1 avocado, pitted, peeled, and sliced

1 egg

1 chipotle chili in adobo sauce 1/4 cup light mayonnaise

1/4 cup plain Greek yogurt

tablespoons fresh lime juice

GOOD STEP BY STEP DIRECTIONS

1. After sprinkling the avocado slices with lime juice, set them aside.
2. Create your breading station after that. In a small bowl, combine all-purpose flour, salt, and pepper. Whisk the egg in another bowl.
3. Last but not least, put your breadcrumbs in a third dish.
4. The avocado slices should first be coated in the flour mixture before being dipped in the egg. Spread the breadcrumbs equally over the avocado pieces.
5. Cook for 11 minutes at 380 degrees F in the preheated Air Fryer while shaking the frying basket halfway through.
6. Blend the chipotle Chile, mayo, and
7. Add the Greek yogurt until the sauce is smooth and creamy in your food processor.
8. Slices of avocado should be served warm with the sauce on the side. Enjoy!

Beef Bites

PREPARATION TIME REQUIRED	
Coking Time:	15 minutes
Servings:	2

INGREDIENTS TO USE

1 teaspoon cayenne pepper 8 oz beef loin, chopped
1 teaspoon apple cider vinegar
¼ teaspoon salt
1 tablespoon coconut flour 1 teaspoon nut oil

GOOD STEP BY STEP DIRECTIONS

1.   Salt and apple cider vinegar should be added to the beef. Then top it with coconut flour and cayenne pepper. Put the meat in the air fryer after giving it a good shake. Add some nut oil and cook it for a few minutes at 365F. To prevent burning, shake the beef popcorn every five minutes.

Tomato & Avocado Egg Rolls

PREPARATION TIME REQUIRED	
Coking Time:	20 minutes
Servings:	5

INGREDIENTS TO USE

Salt and pepper, to taste
3 avocados, peeled and pitted 1 tomato, diced
10 egg roll wrappers

GOOD STEP BY STEP DIRECTIONS

1. Set your Air Fryer to 350°F before using.
2. In a bowl, combine the tomato and avocados. With a fork, mix the ingredients until they are smooth after adding salt and pepper.
3. Distribute the mixture evenly among the wrappers. Wrap the filling completely in the wrappers as you roll them around it.
4. Cook the rolls for 5 minutes after transferring them to a prepared baking pan

Tomatoes & Herbs

PREPARATION TIME REQUIRED	
Coking Time:	30 minutes
Servings:	2

INGREDIENTS TO USE

Cooking spray pepper to taste
Parmesan, grated [optional] Parsley
minced [optional]
2 large tomatoes, washed and cut into halves
Herbs, such as oregano, basil, thyme
 Rosemary, sage to taste

GOOD STEP BY STEP DIRECTIONS

1. Spray a small quantity of cooking spray on both the top and bottom of each tomato half.
2. Sprinkle a little pepper and your preferred herbs over the tomatoes.
3. Put the cut-side-up side of the tomatoes in the basket. Cook for 20 minutes at 0°F, or longer if required.
4. For a cool summer snack, serve hot, at room temperature, or chilled. Before serving, you have the option of adding grated Parmesan
5. and chopped parsley as a garnish.

Oliver Fritters

PREPARATION TIME REQUIRED	
Coking Time:	12 minutes
Servings:	6

INGREDIENTS TO USE

Salt and black pepper to the taste of 3 spring onions, chopped
½ cup kalamata olives pitted
and minced 3 zucchinis, grated
½ cup almond flour
½ cup parsley, chopped 1 egg
Cooking spray

GOOD STEP BY STEP DIRECTIONS

1. Mix all the ingredients in a bowl, excluding the frying spray, and combine thoroughly before forming the mixture into medium-sized fritters. The fritters should be placed in the basket of your air fryer, greased with frying spray, and cooked for 6 minutes on each side at 380 degrees F. As an appetizer, serve them.

Veggie Bread Rolls

PREPARATION TIME REQUIRED	
Coking Time:	33 minutes
Servings:	8

INGREDIENTS TO USE

½ teaspoon ground turmeric Salt, as required
5 large potatoes, peeled
2 tablespoons vegetable oil,
Divide 2 small onions, finely chopped
8 bread slices, trimmed
2 green chilies, seeded and chopped 2 curry leaves

1. The potatoes should be added to a pan of boiling water and cook for 20 minutes or so.
2. Mash the potatoes with a potato masher after thoroughly draining them.

3. One teaspoon of oil should be heated to medium heat in a skillet while the onion is sauteed for four to five minutes.

4. Curry leaves, turmeric, and green chilies should all be added. For roughly one minute, sauté.

5. Mix well after adding the salt and mashed potatoes.

6. Once finished, turn off the heat and let the pan somewhere to cool.

7. From the mixture, form 8 oval-shaped patties of the same size.

8. Completely wet the bread pieces with water.

9. Each piece of bread should be squeezed between your palms to eliminate extra moisture.

10. One patty should be placed in the center of one slice of bread in your palm.

11. To keep the filling in place, roll the bread slice into a spindle and close the edges.

12. Apply some oil to the roll.

13. The remaining slices, filling, and oil should be repeated.

14. Set the Air Fryer to 390 degrees Fahrenheit. Spray cooking oil on the Air Fryer basket to grease it.

15. Rolls should be added in a single layer to the prepared basket.

16. For around 12–13 minutes, air fry.

17. Serve.

Country-style Deviled Eggs

PREPARATION TIME REQUIRED	
Coking Time:	25 minutes
Servings:	8

INGREDIENTS TO USE

1/2 teaspoon Worcestershire sauce
2 tablespoons mayonnaise
teaspoon hot sauce
6 eggs
6 slices bacon
tablespoons green onions,
1 tablespoon pickle relish
Salt and ground black pepper,
to taste 1 teaspoon of smoked paprika

GOOD STEP BY STEP DIRECTIONS

1. Lower the eggs onto a wire rack after placing them in the Air Fryer basket.
2. Cook for 15 minutes at 0 degrees F.
3. To stop the cooking, place them in a bath of freezing water. Slice the eggs in half after peeling them under cold running water.
4. Cook the bacon for 3 minutes at 0 degrees F, then turn it over and cook for another 3. Finally, chop the bacon, and set it aside.
5. The reserved bacon should be added to the mashed egg yolks along with the mayo, spicy sauce, Worcestershire sauce, green onions, pickle relish, salt, and black pepper. The yolk mixture should then be spooned into egg whites.
6. Apply smoked paprika as a garnish. Good appetite!

Chicken Wings in Barbecue Sauce

PREPARATION TIME REQUIRED	
Coking Time:	20 minutes
Servings:	6

INGREDIENTS TO USE

For the Wings:

1/4 cup habanero hot sauce Chopped fresh parsley, or garnish
Pound chicken wings

For the Sauce:

1/4 cup ketchup, no sugar, added 1 garlic clove, minced
Salt and ground black pepper, to your liking 1/8 teaspoon ground allspice
tablespoon apple cider vinegar, 1 tablespoon olive oil
1/4 cup water
1 tablespoon yellow mustard
1/4 teaspoon celery salt

GOOD STEP BY STEP DIRECTIONS

1. Place all the sauce ingredients in a sauté pan and cook over medium-high heat. Bring the sauce to a boil. Then, lower the heat and simmer the mixture until it has thickened.
2. The chicken wings should be cooked for 6 minutes in the air fryer before being turned over and cooked for a further 6 minutes. Celery salt is used to season them.
3. Garnish with fresh parsley leaves and serve with the prepared sauce and habanero spicy sauce. Good appetite!

Spicy Avocado Fries Wrapped in Bacon

PREPARATION TIME REQUIRED	
Coking Time:	10 minutes
Servings:	5

INGREDIENTS TO USE

1 teaspoon ground black pepper

2 avocados, pitted and cut into 10 pieces 1 teaspoon salt

½ teaspoon garlic powder

5 rashers back bacon, cut into halves

2 teaspoons chili powder

GOOD STEP BY STEP DIRECTIONS

1. One avocado slice should be placed on each bacon slice after the rashers have been laid out on a spotless surface. Garlic powder, chili powder, salt, and black pepper should also be added.
2. Then, using the remaining rolls, wrap the bacon slice around the avocado and fasten it with a cocktail stick or toothpick.
3. Set your air fryer to 0 degrees Fahrenheit, cook your food there for 5 minutes, and serve with your favorite dipping sauce.

Potato Wedges

PREPARATION TIME REQUIRED	
Coking Time:	**30 minutes**
Servings:	**4**

INGREDIENTS TO USE

olive oil Pepper to taste Salt to taste
4 medium potatoes, cut into wedges 1 tbsp.
tbsp.
Cajun spice

GOOD STEP BY STEP DIRECTIONS

1. Put the potato wedges and olive oil in the Air Fryer basket.
2. Cook wedges for minutes at 370°F, shaking the basket twice during that time.
3. Place the cooked wedges in a bowl and season with salt, pepper, and Cajun seasoning. Serve hot.

Ranch Dipped Filets

PREPARATION TIME REQUIRED	
Coking Time:	**13 minutes**
Servings:	**2**

INGREDIENTS TO USE

½ packet ranch dressing mix powder 1¼ tablespoons vegetable oil
¼ cup panko breadcrumbs 1 egg beaten
Garnish: Herbs and chilies
tilapia filets

GOOD STEP BY STEP DIRECTIONS

1. Grease the air fryer basket and preheat the air fryer to 350 degrees Fahrenheit.
2. In a bowl, combine panko breadcrumbs and ranch dressing.
3. Fish filets should be dipped in eggs after being whisked in a shallow basin.
4. Place in the Air Fryer basket after dredging in the breadcrumbs.
5. After 13 minutes of cooking,

6.   Garnish with herbs and chilies before serving.

Mozzarella Snack

PREPARATION TIME REQUIRED	
Coking Time:	**8 minutes**
Servings:	**5**

INGREDIENTS TO USE

2 teaspoons psyllium husk powder
¾ cup almond flour
¼ teaspoon sweet paprika
2 cups mozzarella, shredded

GOOD STEP BY STEP DIRECTIONS

1.   Put the mozzarella in a bowl, microwave it for two minutes, then rapidly add the remaining ingredients and combine thoroughly to form a dough. The dough should be divided into two balls, rolled out on two baking sheets, and then cut into triangles. Place the tortillas in the basket of your air fryer, and bake for 5 minutes at 370 degrees F. Put in bowls and provide as a snack.

Asian Teriyaki Chicken

PREPARATION TIME REQUIRED	
Coking Time:	**40 minutes**
Servings:	**6**

INGREDIENTS TO USE

1/2 cup water
1/2 teaspoon five-spice powder 2 tablespoons rice wine vinegar 1/2 teaspoons fresh ginger, tablespoons fresh chives, roughly chopped Teriyaki Sauce:
½ pounds chicken drumettes
Sea salt and cracked black pepper, to taste
tablespoon sesame oil 1/4 cup soy sauce
grated 2 cloves garlic, crushed

GOOD STEP BY STEP DIRECTIONS

2. To begin with, preheat your air fryer to 380 degrees Fahrenheit. Rub salt and freshly cracked black pepper on the chicken drumettes.

3. Cook for around 15 minutes in a preheated Air Fryer. After seven minutes, flip them over and continue cooking.

4. Sesame oil, soy sauce, water, five-spice powder, vinegar, ginger, and garlic are combined in a skillet over medium heat while the chicken drumettes roast. While intermittently stirring, cook for 5 minutes.

5. Lower the heat now, and let it simmer for a while to thicken the glaze.

6. After that, coat the chicken drumettes with the glaze.

7. Continue air-frying for a further 6 minutes, or until the top is crispy. Serve with leftover glaze on top and fresh chives for decoration. Good appetite!

Ricotta Balls

PREPARATION TIME REQUIRED	
Coking Time:	25 minutes
Servings:	2--4

INGREDIENTS TO USE

¼ tsp. pepper powder to taste 1 tsp. orange zest, grated
For coating
2 tbsp. chives, finely chopped
2 tbsp. fresh basil, finely chopped 4 tbsp. flour
¼ tsp. salt to taste
¼ cup friendly bread crumbs 1 tbsp. vegetable oil
cups ricotta, grated 2 eggs, separated

GOOD STEP BY STEP DIRECTIONS

1. Set your Air Fryer to a preheated 390°F.
2. Combine the yolks, flour, chives, salt, and pepper in a bowl. Add the ricotta and mix it in with your hands.
3. Create balls out of an equal amount of the mixture.
4. Combine the oil and bread crumbs until they have a crumbly texture.
5. After dredging the balls in the bread crumbs, place each one in the basket of the fryer.
6. Place the fryer's basket inside. Until the food is golden brown, air fry for 8 minutes.
7. Offer a sauce of your choice, such as ketchup.

Pita Bread Cheese Pizza

PREPARATION TIME REQUIRED	
Coking Time:	6 minutes
Servings:	4

INGREDIENTS TO USE

½ teaspoon fresh garlic, minced
1 pita bread
¼ cup sausage
1 tablespoon yellow onion,
1 tablespoon of pizza sauce
¼ cup Mozzarella cheese 7 slices pepperoni
drizzle extra-virgin olive oil

GOOD STEP BY STEP DIRECTIONS

1. Grease the air fryer basket and preheat the air fryer to 350 degrees Fahrenheit.
2. On the pita bread, spread pizza sauce,
3. then top with cheese, sausages, pepperoni, onions, and garlic.
4. Place it in the Air Fryer basket and drizzle with olive oil.
5. Cook for approximately 6 minutes before serving warm.

Brussels Sprouts

PREPARATION TIME REQUIRED	
Coking Time:	15 minutes
Servings:	2

INGREDIENTS TO USE

tbsp. Olive oil

¼ tsp. salt

Cup Brussels sprouts, sliced in half 1 tbsp. balsamic vinegar

GOOD STEP BY STEP DIRECTIONS

1. 1. Combine the ingredients in a bowl, being sure to thoroughly coat the Brussels sprouts.
2. 2. Put the sprouts in the air fryer basket and cook for 10 minutes at 400°F, shaking the basket halfway through.

Puppy Poppers

PREPARATION TIME REQUIRED	
Coking Time:	25 minutes
Servings:	50 Treats

INGREDIENTS TO USE

1 cup flour

tsp. baking powder

cup oats

½ cup unsweetened apple sauce

1 cup peanut butter

GOOD STEP BY STEP DIRECTIONS

1. In a bowl, mix the peanut butter and applesauce to a smooth consistency.
2. Add the flour, baking powder, and oats. Once a soft dough is formed, continue mixing.
3. Create a ball out of a half-teaspoon of dough, then repeat with the remaining dough.

4. Set the Air Fryer to 350°F in advance.
5. Oil should be applied to the basket's bottom.
6. In the fryer, add the poppers, and cook for 8 minutes, turning the balls over halfway through. The poppers might need to be prepared in batches.
7. Serve the poppers right away, or store them in an airtight container for up to two weeks. Let the poppers cool.

Flavorful Pork Meatballs

PREPARATION TIME REQUIRED	
Coking Time:	10 minutes
Servings:	4

INGREDIENTS TO USE

2 tbsp fresh mint, chopped 1/2 tbsp cilantro, chopped

2 tsp red pepper flakes, crushed 1 1/2 tbsp butter, melted

1/2 lb ground pork

garlic cloves, minced

1 tsp kosher salt

eggs, lightly beaten 2 tbsp capers

GOOD STEP BY STEP DIRECTIONS

1. 395 F, preheat the air fryer.
2. All components should be added to the mixing bowl and thoroughly mixed.
3. Spray cooking spray in the air fryer basket.
4. From the meat mixture, form little balls that you can drop into the air fryer basket.
5. For 10 minutes, cook the meatballs. Halfway through, shake the basket.
6. Enjoy after serving.

Veggie Cream Stuff Mushrooms

PREPARATION TIME REQUIRED

Coking Time:	8 minutes
Servings:	12

INGREDIENTS TO USE

24 oz mushrooms, cut stems 1/2 cup sour cream
cup cheddar cheese, shredded 1 small carrot, diced
1/2 bell pepper, diced 1/2 onion, diced
bacon slices, diced

GOOD STEP BY STEP DIRECTIONS

1. Finely chop the mushroom stems.
2. Apply cooking spray to the pan and warm it up over medium heat.
3. Cook until the chopped mushrooms, bacon, carrot, onion, and bell pepper.
4. Take the pan off the heat. Stir thoroughly after adding the cheese and sour cream to the cooked veggies.
5. Place the mushroom cap with the veggie mixture inside before placing it in the air fryer basket.
6. For 8 minutes, cook mushrooms at 350 F.
7. Enjoy after serving.

Onion Dip

PREPARATION TIME REQUIRED	
Coking Time:	25 minutes
Servings:	8

INGREDIENTS TO USE

Salt
6 tbsp butter, softened pepper
2 lbs. onion, chopped 1/2 tsp baking soda

GOOD STEP BY STEP DIRECTIONS

1. In a pan over medium heat, melt the butter.
2. Sauté for five minutes after adding the onion and baking soda.
3. Place the onion mixture in the baking dish for the air fryer.
4. Cook for 25 minutes at 370 F in the air fryer.
5. Enjoy after serving.

Mini Cheeseburger Bites

PREPARATION TIME REQUIRED	
Coking Time:	20 minutes
Servings:	4

INGREDIENTS TO USE

1 ½ teaspoons minced green garlic 1/2 teaspoon cumin
tablespoon Dijon mustard
Salt and ground black pepper, to savor 12 cherry tomatoes
tablespoons minced scallions 1 pound ground beef
12 cubes of cheddar cheese

GOOD STEP BY STEP DIRECTIONS

1. Use your hands or a spatula to thoroughly combine the mustard, ground beef, cumin, scallions, garlic, salt, and pepper in a sizable mixing bowl.
2. Form into 1 meatball, then cook in an air fryer that has been prepared to 375

degrees F for 15 minutes. Cook them in the air fryer until the center is done. Cocktail sticks with cheese, cherry tomatoes, and tiny burgers should be used. Good appetite!

Lemon Tofu Cubes

PREPARATION TIME REQUIRED	
Coking Time:	7 minutes
Servings:	2

INGREDIENTS TO USE

1 teaspoon lemon juice
½ teaspoon ground coriander 1 tablespoon avocado oil
½ teaspoon chili flakes 6 oz tofu

GOOD STEP BY STEP DIRECTIONS

1. Combine the ground coriander, avocado oil, lemon juice, and chili flakes in a small basin. Slice the tofu into cubes, then mix the coriander. Make the tofu shake. The tofu cubes should then be placed in the air fryer, which has been preheated to 400F. For 4 minutes, cook the tofu.
2. After that, turn the tofu over and cook it for an additional three minutes.

Cheddar Cheese Breadsticks

PREPARATION TIME REQUIRED	
Coking Time:	30 minutes
Servings:	6

INGREDIENTS TO USE

6 ounces mature Cheddar, cold, freshly grated 2 tablespoons cream cheese
tablespoons cold butter
1/2 teaspoon celery seeds
1/2 cup almond meal
Sea salt and ground black pepper, to taste
1/4 teaspoon smoked paprika

GOOD STEP BY STEP DIRECTIONS

1. 1.To begin, preheat your air fryer to 330 degrees Fahrenheit. With parchment paper, line the Air Fryer basket.
2. 2. Thoroughly combine the almond meal, celery seeds, paprika, salt, and black pepper in a mixing dish.
3. 3. Next, put the cheese and butter in a stand mixer's bowl. Add the almond meal mixture slowly while stirring, then thoroughly blend.
4. 4. After that, fill a cookie press with batter and attach a star disk to it. On the parchment paper, pipe the long dough ribbons in various patterns. After that, cut the lengths into six.
5. 5. Bake for one minute in the preheated Air Fryer.
6. 6. Carry out step 6 with the remaining dough. On a rack, let the cheese straws cool. You can keep them in an airtight jar sandwiched between sheets of parchment. Good appetite

Easy Habanero Wings

PREPARATION TIME REQUIRED	
Coking Time:	25 minutes
Servings:	6

INGREDIENTS TO USE

1 teaspoon freshly ground black pepper, or to taste
1 teaspoon smoked cayenne pepper
1 ½ pounds chicken wings 1 teaspoon garlic salt
cloves garlic, peeled and halved 2 tablespoons habanero hot sauce
1/2 tablespoon soy sauce

GOOD STEP BY STEP DIRECTIONS

1. The chicken wings should be garlicked. Then, add salt, black pepper, and smoked cayenne pepper to season them.
2. Add the soy sauce, habanero hot sauce, and honey to the food basket with the chicken wings and toss to coat evenly on both sides.
3. The chicken wings should be heated through after 16 minutes of air-frying at 5 degrees F.
4.

Bacon and Roasted Brussels Sprouts

PREPARATION TIME REQUIRED	
Coking Time:	45 minutes
Servings:	2

INGREDIENTS TO USE

¼ cup fish sauce
24 oz brussels sprouts
¼ cup bacon grease 6 strips bacon Pepper to taste

GOOD STEP BY STEP DIRECTIONS

1. The Brussels sprouts should be quartered and stemmed.

2. Combine them with the fish sauce and bacon fat.
3. Cook the bacon by cutting it into thin slices.
4. The sprouts should also have pepper and bacon.
5. Spread out on a greased pan and cook for 35 minutes at 4°F/230°C.
6. About every five minutes, stir.
7. Serve after a few more minutes of broiling.

Sesame Okra

PREPARATION TIME REQUIRED	
Coking Time:	4 minutes
Servings:	4

INGREDIENTS TO USE

1 tsp sesame seeds 1 tbsp sesame oil 1/4 tsp pepper

11 oz okra, wash and chop 1 egg, lightly beaten

1/2 tsp salt

GOOD STEP BY STEP DIRECTIONS

1.   1. Combine the egg, salt, and pepper in a bowl.
2.   2. Stir okra into the egg mixture. Sprinkle sesame seeds on top.
3.   3. Turn the air fryer on at 400 F.
4.   4. Give the okra a good stir. Spray cooking spray in the air fryer basket.
5.   5. Put the cut-up okra in the air fryer basket and cook for 4 minutes.
6.   6. Present and savor.

Vegetable Fritters

PREPARATION TIME REQUIRED	
Coking Time:	15 minutes
Servings:	4

INGREDIENTS TO USE

¾ cup Cheddar cheese, grated

½ tbsp. fresh chopped cilantro 1 egg, whisked

¼ cup flour

¼ cup cooked quinoa

1 cup bell peppers, deveined and chopped 1 tsp. sea salt flakes

1 tsp. cumin

¼ tsp. paprika

½ cup shallots, chopped 2 cloves garlic, minced

GOOD STEP BY STEP DIRECTIONS

1. All the components should be thoroughly mixed in a bowl.
2. Make equal parts of the ingredients and roll each one into a ball. To create patties, lightly press each ball into the palm of your hand.
3. Spray cooking spray on the patties sparingly.
4. With care to avoid overlap, place the patties in the cooking basket of your Air Fryer.
5. Cook for 10 minutes at 340°F, flipping them over halfway through.

Wonton Sausage Appetizers

PREPARATION TIME REQUIRED	
Coking Time:	20 minutes
Servings:	5

INGREDIENTS TO USE

1 egg, whisked with 1 tablespoon of water

1/2 tablespoon fish sauce 1 teaspoon Sriracha sauce 20 wonton wrappers

1/2-pound ground sausage

tablespoons scallions,

chopped 1 garlic clove, minced

GOOD STEP BY STEP DIRECTIONS

1. Combine the ground sausage, scallions, garlic, fish sauce, and Sriracha in a mixing bowl.
2. The mixture should be divided among the wonton wrappers. Put some egg wash on your fingers.
3. The wonton is folded in half. Bring the wontons' two ends together, and then use the egg wash to seal the joints. Each wonton should have its edges pinched before being egg-washed.
4. Put the folded wontons in the cooking basket that has been lightly oiled. Cook for 10 minutes at 360 degrees Fahrenheit. Work in batches, then warm serve. Good appetite!

Shrimps Cakes

PREPARATION TIME REQUIRED	
Coking Time:	5 minutes
Servings:	4

INGREDIENTS TO USE

tablespoons almond flour 1 teaspoon olive oil
1 teaspoon chives
teaspoon dill, chopped 1 teaspoon Psyllium husk
10 oz shrimp, chopped 1 egg, beaten

GOOD STEP BY STEP DIRECTIONS

1. Combine the shrimp, egg, dill, psyllium husk, almond flour, and chives in a mixing dish. Make 4 cakes after the mixture is homogeneous. Set the air fryer to 400F for frying.
2. Sprinkle olive oil over the cakes before placing them in the air fryer. For five minutes, prepare dinner.

Bacon-wrapped Shrimp

PREPARATION TIME REQUIRED	
Coking Time:	7 minutes
Servings:	6

INGREDIENTS TO USE

1 pound bacon, sliced thinly
1 pound shrimp,
peeled and deveined Salt, to taste

GOOD STEP BY STEP DIRECTIONS

GOOD STEP BY STEP DIRECTIONS

1. Grease an air fryer basket and preheat the air fryer to 390 degrees Fahrenheit.
2. 2. Completely enclose 1 shrimp in bacon slices.
3. 3. Carry out step 3 with the remaining bacon and shrimp slices.
4. 4. Arrange the shrimp that have been wrapped in bacon in a baking tray and freeze for approximately 15 minutes.
5. 5. Cook the shrimp for around 7 minutes in an air fryer basket.
6. 6. Remove the dish and serve it hot.

Saucy Chicken Wings with Sage

PREPARATION TIME REQUIRED	
Coking Time:	10 minutes
Servings:	4

INGREDIENTS TO USE

1/3 cup almond flour 1/3 cup buttermilk
1 ½ pound chicken wings 1 tablespoon tamari sauce
1/3 teaspoon fresh sage
teaspoon mustard seeds 1/2 teaspoon garlic paste
1/2 teaspoon freshly ground mixed peppercorns
1/2 teaspoon seasoned salt
teaspoons fresh basil

GOOD STEP BY STEP DIRECTIONS

1. In a sizable mixing bowl, combine the seasonings, garlic paste, chicken wings, buttermilk, and tamari sauce. Drain the wings after about 55 minutes of soaking.
2. Place the wings in the frying basket of the Air Fryer after dredging them in the almond flour.

3. 16 minutes of air-frying at 5 degrees F. Serve with a dressing on the side and a good serving plate. Good appetite!

Crispy Prawns

PREPARATION TIME REQUIRED	
Coking Time:	8 minutes
Servings:	4

INGREDIENTS TO USE

½ pound nacho chips,
1 egg
crushed 18 prawns, peeled and deveined

GOOD STEP BY STEP DIRECTIONS

1. Crack the egg into a shallow dish, and then beat it well.
2. In another dish, place the crumbled nacho chips.
3. Now, coat the prawn with nacho chips after dipping it in the beaten egg.
4. Set the Air Fryer to 355 degrees Fahrenheit.
5. Put the prawns in a single layer in an Air Fryer basket.
6. For around 8 minutes, air fry.
7. Serve warm.

Granny's Green Beans

PREPARATION TIME REQUIRED	
Coking Time:	10 minutes
Servings:	4

INGREDIENTS TO USE

cloves garlic,
minced 1 cup of toasted pine nuts
1 cup butter
lb green beans, trimmed

GOOD STEP BY STEP DIRECTIONS

1. Put some water on to boil.
2. Green beans should be added and cooked for 5 minutes or until soft.
3. In a sizable skillet over high heat, melt the butter.
4. Pine nuts should be lightly browned after 2 minutes of adding the garlic and adding the pine nuts.
5. Green beans should be added to the skillet and turned to coat.

6. Serve!

Pickled Bacon Bowls

PREPARATION TIME REQUIRED	
Coking Time:	20 minutes
Servings:	4

INGREDIENTS TO USE

4 dill pickle spears,
sliced in half and quartered 8 bacon slices, halved, 1 cup avocado mayonnaise

GOOD STEP BY STEP DIRECTIONS

1. Each pickle spear should be wrapped in a bacon slice before being placed in the air fryer basket and cooked for 20 minutes at 400 degrees F.
2. As a snack, divide into bowls and top with mayonnaise.

Tomato Smokies

PREPARATION TIME REQUIRED	
Coking Time:	10 minutes
Servings:	10

INGREDIENTS TO USE

1 teaspoon avocado oil
12 oz pork and beef smokies 3 oz bacon, sliced
½ teaspoon cayenne pepper
1 teaspoon keto tomato sauce 1 teaspoon Erythritol

GOOD STEP BY STEP DIRECTIONS

1. Cayenne pepper and tomato sauce should be added to the smokies. Olive oil and erythritol are then sprinkled over them.
2. After that, wrap the bacon around each smoke and fasten it with a toothpick. Set the air fryer to 400F for frying.
3. The bacon smokies should be cooked in the air fryer for a few minutes. To prevent burning, gently shake them while they are cooking.

Scallops And Bacon Kabobs

PREPARATION TIME REQUIRED	
Coking Time:	40 minutes
Servings:	6

INGREDIENTS TO USE

1/2-pound bacon, diced 1 shallot, diced
1 teaspoon garlic powder 1 teaspoon paprika
Sea salt and ground black pepper, to taste
1 pound sea scallops 1/2 cup coconut milk
1 tablespoon vermouth

GOOD STEP BY STEP DIRECTIONS

1. Sea scallops, coconut milk, vermouth, salt, and black pepper should all be combined in a ceramic bowl and let to marinate for 30 minutes.
2. Place the scallops, bacon, and shallots on the skewers in that order. All over the skewers, sprinkling paprika and garlic powder.
3. Bake for 6 minutes at 400 degrees Fahrenheit in the preheated air fryer. Enjoy warm servings!

Cocktail Sausage and Veggies on A Stick

PREPARATION TIME REQUIRED	
Coking Time:	25 minutes
Servings:	4

INGREDIENTS TO USE

1 red bell pepper, cut into 1 ½-inch piece
16 cocktail sausages, halved 16 pearl onions
1/2 cup tomato chili sauce
green bell pepper,
cut into 1 ½-inch pieces of Salt
and cracked black pepper, to taste

GOOD STEP BY STEP DIRECTIONS

1. On skewers, alternately thread cocktail sausages, pearl onions, and peppers. Add some black and salt pepper.
2. Cook the skewers for 15 minutes at 380 degrees in the preheated Air Fryer, turning them over once or twice to achieve equal cooking.
3. The tomato chili sauce should be served separately. Enjoy!

Aromatic Kale Chips

PREPARATION TIME REQUIRED	
Coking Time:	5 minutes
Servings:	4

INGREDIENTS TO USE

1 1/2 teaspoons seasoned salt
1 ½ teaspoon garlic powder
½ tablespoons olive oil
1 bunch of kale, torn into small pieces
2 tablespoons lemon juice

1. Kale should be combined with the other ingredients.
2. Cook for 4 to 5 minutes at 195 degrees F, stirring the kale halfway through.
3. Serve with the dipping sauce of your choice.

DESSERTS RECIPES

Vanilla Orange Custard

PREPARATION TIME REQUIRED

Coking Time:	35 minutes
Servings:	6

INGREDIENTS TO USE

2 teaspoons vanilla paste 1/4 cup fresh orange juice

eggs

1/2 cup swerve

1/2 teaspoon orange rind, grated 1 ½ cardamom pods, bruised

ounces cream cheese, at room temperature

2 ½ cans condensed milk, sweetened

GOOD STEP BY STEP DIRECTIONS

1. Swerve must be melted in a pot over a moderate temperature for about 12 minutes. Pour the melted sugar into the six ramekins quickly but gently, tilting them to coat the bottoms, and then give them a moment to cool.
2. Beat the cheese in a mixing bowl until it's smooth. Add each egg one at a time, and beat until it's pale and creamy.
3. Remix after adding the milk, cardamom, vanilla, orange juice, and orange rind. On top of the caramelized sugar, pour the mixture. Cook for 28 minutes at 5 degrees F while air-frying it undercover.
4. After being chilled for the night, decorate with berries or other fruits before serving.

Boozy Baileys Fudge Brownies

PREPARATION TIME REQUIRED	
Coking Time:	35 minutes
Servings:	8

INGREDIENTS TO USE

ounces unsweetened chocolate chips 1/2 cup sour cream

1/3 cup powdered erythritol

tablespoons unsweetened cocoa powder, sifted 1/2 cup almond flour

tablespoons Baileys

cup granulated swerve

1/2 cup coconut flour 1/4 teaspoon salt

1/4 teaspoon baking powder

ounces Ricotta cheese, room temperature

1/2 cup butter, melted then cooled 2 eggs room temperature

teaspoon vanilla

GOOD STEP BY STEP DIRECTIONS

1. Mix flour, cocoa powder, salt, baking powder, and granulated sugar well in a mixing basin.
2. Add vanilla, eggs, and butter. Fill a baking pan with the batter after lightly greasing it.
3. 25 minutes of air-frying at 5 degrees F. Place them on a wire rack and let them cool somewhat.
4. Once the chocolate chips are completely melted in the microwave, let the mixture cool to room temperature.
5. When everything is combined, add the Ricotta cheese, Baileys, sour cream, and powdered erythritol.
6. This mixture should be applied to the brownie's top. Serve cold if possible.

Chocolate Cake

PREPARATION TIME REQUIRED	
Coking Time:	40 minutes
Servings:	4

INGREDIENTS TO USE

For cake:

in a bowl, sift together the flour, baking powder,
and cocoa powder.

For Cake:

1/3 cup plain flour

¼ teaspoon baking powder

1½ tablespoons unsweetened cocoa powder 2 egg yolks

½ ounce caster sugar

2 tablespoons vegetable oil 3¾ tablespoons milk

teaspoon vanilla extract For Meringue:

egg whites

1-ounce caster sugar

1/8 teaspoon cream of tartar

GOOD STEP BY STEP DIRECTIONS

1. Add the remaining ingredients to another bowl and whisk to incorporate.
2. Add the flour mixture and stir thoroughly.
3. For the meringue, combine all the ingredients in a clean glass bowl and beat vigorously with an electric mixer until stiff peaks form.
4. Mix the flour and the remaining 1/3 of the meringue well with a hand whisker.
5. The rest of the meringue is folded in.
6. Set the air fryer to 355 degrees Fahrenheit.
7. Put the ingredients in a chiffon pan that has not been oiled.
8. Cover the pan completely with a piece of foil, then use a fork to make some holes in it.
9. In a basket for an air fryer, arrange the cake pan.
10. Now, set the air fryer's temperature to 320 degrees Fahrenheit.
11. For roughly 30-35 minutes, air fry.
12. Set the temperature to 285 degrees F after removing the foil.
13. A toothpick inserted in the center should come out clean after another 5

minutes of air frying.

14. Place the cake pan on a wire rack after removing it from the air fryer to cool for about 10 minutes.

15. After that, flip the cake over onto a wire rack to finish cooling before slicing.

16. Slice the cake however you choose and serve.

Coconut Cheese Cookies

PREPARATION TIME REQUIRED	
Coking Time:	12 minutes
Servings:	30

INGREDIENTS TO USE

¾ cup coconut flakes 1 cup swerve

8 oz cream cheese 1 tsp vanilla

tbsp baking powder

¾ cup butter,

softened 1 ¼ cup coconut flour Pinch of salt

GOOD STEP BY STEP DIRECTIONS

1. Set the air fryer to 325 F before using it.
2. Using a hand mixer, whip up the cream cheese, butter, and sweetener in a bowl.
3. Stir in the vanilla thoroughly.
4. Salt, baking powder, and coconut flour should all be added. Mix thoroughly.
5. Coconut flakes are added; blend.
6. From the mixture, bake cookies, then arrange them on a dish.
7. Cook for 12 minutes with batches of cookies in the air fryer.
8. Prepare and consume.

Yummy Brownies

PREPARATION TIME REQUIRED	
Coking Time:	10 minutes
Servings:	4

INGREDIENTS TO USE

1/2 tsp vanilla

2 tbsp unsweetened applesauce 1 tsp liquid stevia

1 tbsp coconut oil, melted 3 tbsp almond flour

1 tbsp unsweetened almond milk

1/2 cup almond butter

1/4 tsp sea salt

tbsp cocoa powder 1/4 tsp baking powder
1/2 tsp baking soda

GOOD STEP BY STEP DIRECTIONS

1. Set the air fryer to 350 degrees.
2. Cooking spray should be used to grease the baking pan for the air fryer.
3. Almond flour, baking soda, cocoa powder, baking powder, and salt should all be combined in a small bowl. Place aside.
4. Melt the coconut oil and almond butter in a small bowl in the microwave.
5. Stir well after adding the sugar, vanilla, almond milk, and applesauce to the coconut oil mixture.
6. Mix the dry ingredients with the wet components after adding them.
7. Pour the batter into the prepared dish, and cook for 10 minutes in the air fryer.
8. Slice, then dish. Set the air fryer to 350 degrees.
9. Cooking spray should be used to grease the baking pan for the air fryer.
10. Almond flour, baking soda, cocoa powder, baking powder, and salt should all be combined in a small bowl. Place aside.
11. Melt the coconut oil and almond butter in a small bowl in the microwave.
12. Stir well after adding the sugar, vanilla, almond milk, and applesauce to the coconut oil mixture.
13. Mix the dry ingredients with the wet components after adding them.
14. Pour the batter into the prepared dish, and cook for 10 minutes in the air fryer.
15. Slice, then dish.

Clove Crackers

PREPARATION TIME REQUIRED

Coking Time:	33 minutes
Servings:	8

INGREDIENTS TO USE

½ teaspoon ground clove 2 tablespoons Erythritol
1 teaspoon xanthan gum 1 teaspoon flax meal
3 tablespoons coconut oil, softened
1 cup almond flour
½ teaspoon salt
1 teaspoon baking powder 1 teaspoon lemon juice
1 egg, beaten

GOOD STEP BY STEP DIRECTIONS

1. Almond flour, xanthan gum, flax meal, salt, baking powder, and ground clove should all be combined in a mixing dish. Add coconut oil, lemon juice, egg, and erythritol. With the aid of a fork, carefully stir the mixture. After that, knead the mixture until a soft dough forms. Put parchment down to cover the cutting board. Roll up the dough into a thin layer after placing it on the parchment. Square up the thin dough (crackers). the air fryer to 360F before using. With baking paper, line the air fryer basket. The prepared crackers should be cooked in the air fryer basket in a single layer for a few minutes, or until they are dry and light brown. With the remaining uncooked crackers, repeat the same procedures.

Peach Pie Recipe

PREPARATION TIME REQUIRED	
Coking Time:	45 minutes
Servings:	4

INGREDIENTS TO USE

tbsp. lemon juice 1/2 cup sugar

¼ lbs. peaches; pitted and chopped.

2 tbsp. cornstarch

A pinch of nutmeg; ground 2 tbsp. butter; melted

1 tbsp. dark rum

tbsp. flour

pie dough

GOOD STEP BY STEP DIRECTIONS

2. Pie dough should be rolled into a pie pan that fits your air fryer and firmly pressed.
3. Peaches, sugar, flour, nutmeg, rum, lemon juice, and butter should all be combined in a bowl with the peaches.
4. This should be poured and distributed into a pie pan. Cook for 35 minutes at 0 °F in an air fryer. Serve hot or chilly

Apple Wedges

PREPARATION TIME REQUIRED	
Coking Time:	**25 minutes**
Servings:	**4**

INGREDIENTS TO USE

½ tsp. ground cinnamon

½ cup dried apricots, chopped 1 – 2 tbsp. sugar

4 large apples 2 tbsp. olive oil

GOOD STEP BY STEP DIRECTIONS

1. The apples should be peeled and cut into eight wedges. Discard the cores.
2. Apply the oil to the apple slices.
3. Each wedge should be cooked in the Air Fryer for 12 to 15 minutes at 0°F.
4. Add the apricots and simmer for a further three minutes.
5. Cinnamon and sugar are combined. Before serving, top the cooked apples with this mixture.

Chocolate And Peanut Butter Fondants

PREPARATION TIME REQUIRED	
Coking Time:	**25 minutes**
Servings:	**4**

INGREDIENTS TO USE

⅛ cup flour sieved 1 tsp salt

4 eggs, room temperature

¼ cup water cooking spray

½ cup peanut butter,

crunchy 2 tbsp butter, diced

¼ cup + ¼ cup sugar

GOOD STEP BY STEP DIRECTIONS

1. To put on top of the chocolate fondant, make a salted praline. A saucepan should have 1/4 cup sugar, a teaspoon of salt, and water. Over low heat, stir and bring it to a boil. Simmer for the intended color's reduction and

attainment. It should cool and firm after being poured into a baking tray.

2. Set the air fryer's temperature to 300 F.

3. Place a heatproof bowl on top of a saucepan of medium-heat water. Butter, peanut butter, and chocolate should be added. Until everything is completely melted, blended, and smooth, stir continuously. Remove the bowl and give it some time to cool. Whisk the eggs into the chocolate. Mix in the remaining sugar and flour.

4. Spread cooking spray on tiny loaf pans, then divide the chocolate mixture among them. Cook for 7 minutes with 2 pans in the basket at a time. Take them out, and then serve the fondants with a salted praline.

Tea Cookies

PREPARATION TIME REQUIRED	
Coking Time:	25 minutes
Servings:	15

INGREDIENTS TO USE

1 teaspoon organic vanilla extract

1 teaspoon ground cinnamon 2 teaspoons sugar

½ cup salted butter, softened

2 cups almond meal 1 organic egg

GOOD STEP BY STEP DIRECTIONS

1. Grease an air fryer basket and preheat the air fryer to 370 degrees Fahrenheit.
2. All the ingredients should be thoroughly mixed in a bowl.
3. From the mixture, form balls of the same size and place them in the air fryer basket.
4. After about five minutes, push each ball down with a fork.
5. Cook the cookies for about 20 minutes, then let them cool before serving them with tea.

Molten Lava Cake

PREPARATION TIME REQUIRED	
Coking Time:	20 minutes
Servings:	4

INGREDIENTS TO USE

½ oz dark chocolate melted 2 eggs
1 ½ tbsp self-rising flour
3 ½ tbsp sugar

GOOD STEP BY STEP DIRECTIONS

1. 4 ramekins should be butter-greased. Beat the eggs and sugar until foamy and preheat the air fryer to 375 F. Butter and chocolate are added after a gentle fold of flour.
2. The mixture should be divided among the ramekins and baked in the air fryer for a few minutes.
3. Before inverting the lava cakes upside down onto serving dishes, allow them cool for 2 minutes.

Peanut Cookies

PREPARATION TIME REQUIRED	
Coking Time:	5 minutes
Servings:	4

INGREDIENTS TO USE

¼ teaspoon vanilla extract
egg, beaten
tablespoons peanut butter
4 teaspoons Erythritol

GOOD STEP BY STEP DIRECTIONS

1. Combine the peanut butter, erythritol, egg, and vanilla extract in a mixing dish. Utilizing a fork, stir the mixture.
2. Make 4 cookies next. the air fryer to 355F before using. The cookies should be cooked for 5 minutes in the air fryer.

Chocolate Custard

PREPARATION TIME REQUIRED	
Coking Time:	32 minutes
Servings:	4

INGREDIENTS TO USE

cup of unsweetened almond milk
tbsp unsweetened cocoa powder
1/4 cup Swerve
1 tsp vanilla
eggs
1 cup heavy whipping cream
Pinch of salt

GOOD STEP BY STEP DIRECTIONS

the air fryer to 305 F before using.
Blend all items in the blender after adding them.
Put the ramekins in the air fryer after pouring the ingredients into them.
For 32 minutes, cook.
Enjoy after serving.

Nutty Fudge Muffins

PREPARATION TIME REQUIRED	
Coking Time:	10 minutes
Servings:	10

INGREDIENTS TO USE

¼ cup walnuts, chopped 1/3 cup vegetable oil
teaspoons water
package fudge brownie mixes 1 egg

GOOD STEP BY STEP DIRECTIONS

1. Lightly grease muffin tins and preheat the air fryer to 300 degrees Fahrenheit.
2. In a bowl, combine the brownie mix, egg, oil, and water.
3. After incorporating the walnuts, spoon the mixture into the muffin tins.

4. Cook the muffin tins for around 10 minutes after placing them in the Air Fryer basket.
5. Remove the dish and serve right away.

Banana Cake

PREPARATION TIME REQUIRED	
Coking Time:	40 minutes
Servings:	6

INGREDIENTS TO USE

½ cup vegetable oil 2 eggs
¼ cup walnuts, chopped
½ teaspoon vanilla extract
3 medium bananas, peeled and mashed
¼ cup raisins, chopped
1 teaspoon baking soda
½ teaspoon ground cinnamon Salt, to taste
½ cup sugar
1½ cups cake flour

GOOD STEP BY STEP DIRECTIONS

1. Mix the flour, baking soda, cinnamon, and salt in a large bowl.
2. Beat the eggs and oil thoroughly in another basin.
3. Bananas, vanilla bean essence, and sugar are added. Blend thoroughly by whisking.
4. Stir briefly after adding the flour mixture.
5. Set the air fryer to 320 degrees Fahrenheit. Butter a cake pans.
6. Mixture should be distributed equally into the prepared cake pan. Add walnuts and raisins on top.
7. Put some foil over the pan and seal it.
8. In a basket for an air fryer, arrange the cake pan.
9. Now, set the air fryer's temperature to 300 degrees Fahrenheit.
10. For around 30 minutes, air fry.
11. Set the temperature to 285 degrees F after removing the foil.
12. A toothpick inserted in the center should come out clean after another 5 to 10 minutes of air frying.
13. Place the cake pan on a wire rack after removing it from the air fryer to cool

for about 10 minutes.

14. After that, flip the cake over onto a wire rack to finish cooling before slicing.

15. Slice the cake however you choose and serve.

Flavorsome Peach Cake

PREPARATION TIME REQUIRED	
Coking Time:	40 minutes
Servings:	6

INGREDIENTS TO USE

1/8 teaspoon salt 1/2 cup caster sugar 2 eggs

1/4 teaspoon freshly grated nutmeg

1/2 teaspoon baking powder

1 ¼ cups cake flour

1/2 teaspoon orange extract

1/2-pound peaches, pitted and mashed

3 tablespoons honey

1 teaspoon pure vanilla extract 1/4

teaspoon ground cinnamon 1/3 cup ghee

GOOD STEP BY STEP DIRECTIONS

1. The air fryer should first be preheated to 3 degrees F. Spray a nonstick cooking spray on the cake pan.
2. Cream the ghee and caster sugar together in a mixing basin. Add the egg, honey, and mashed peaches after that.
3. After combining the remaining ingredients, whisk in the peach/honey mixture to create the cake batter.
4. Now, pour the prepared batter into the cake pan and use a spoon to level the top.
5. A tester inserted in the center of your cake should come out fully dry after 3 minutes of baking. Enjoy!

Hazelnut Brownie Cups

PREPARATION TIME REQUIRED	
Coking Time:	30 minutes
Servings:	12

INGREDIENTS TO USE

tsp. pure vanilla extract

large eggs

¼ cup of red wine

6 oz. semisweet chocolate chips

stick butter, at room temperature

tbsp. cocoa powder

¼ tsp. hazelnut extract

½ cup ground hazelnuts Pinch of kosher salt

1 cup sugar

¾ cup flour

GOOD STEP BY STEP DIRECTIONS

1. Microwave the butter and chocolate chips until they are melted.
2. Whisk the sugar, eggs, red wine, hazelnuts, and vanilla essence together in a big bowl. the chocolate mixture in.
3. Once a creamy, smooth consistency is attained, whisk in the flour, cocoa powder, ground hazelnuts, and a dash of kosher salt.
4. Put cupcake liners in each of the muffin tin cups. Fill each one with an equal amount of the batter.
5. Cook in batches as necessary and air bake for 28 to 30 minutes at 360°F.
6. If desired, top the dish with ganache.

Plum Bars Recipe

PREPARATION TIME REQUIRED	
Coking Time:	26 minutes
Servings:	8

INGREDIENTS TO USE

1 cup brown sugar 1/2 tsp. baking soda

2 tbsp. butter; melted 1 egg; whisked

2 cups rolled oats

1 tsp. cinnamon powder cooking spray

2 cups dried plums 6 tbsp. water

GOOD STEP BY STEP DIRECTIONS

1. Combine plums and water in your food processor, and process until you get a sticky spread.
2. Oats, cinnamon, baking soda, sugar, egg,
3. and butter should all be combined in a bowl and thoroughly whisked.
4. Spread plum mixture in an air fryer-compatible baking pan that has been sprayed with cooking oil, then press half of the oat's mixture into it. Finally, top with the remaining grain mixture.
5. Introduce the ingredients to your air fryer and cook for 16 minutes at 350 °F. Set the mixture aside to cool before cutting it into medium bars to serve.

Cobbler

PREPARATION TIME REQUIRED	
Coking Time:	30 minutes
Servings:	4

INGREDIENTS TO USE

¼ cup hazelnuts, chopped
¼ cup heavy cream 1 egg, beaten
teaspoon vanilla extract
tablespoons butter softened
½ cup almond flour

GOOD STEP BY STEP DIRECTIONS

1. Combine butter, almond flour, almond flour, vanilla essence, and heavy cream.
2. The mixture is then gently whisked. Set the air fryer to 325F for frying. Use baking paper to line the air fryer pan. Half of the mixture should be poured into the baking pan, carefully pressed down, and topped with hazelnuts. Then, put the pan in the air fryer and pour the remaining batter on top of the hazelnuts.
3. The cobbler needs 30 minutes to cook.

Classic Buttermilk Biscuits

PREPARATION TIME REQUIRED	
Coking Time:	8 minutes
Servings:	4

INGREDIENTS TO USE

¼ cup + 2 tablespoons butter, cut into cubes
¾ teaspoon baking powder
¾ cup buttermilk
1¼ cups all-purpose flour
1 teaspoon granulated sugar Salt, to taste
½ cup cake flour

GOOD STEP BY STEP DIRECTIONS

1. Lightly grease a pie pan and preheat the air fryer to 400 degrees.
2. In a sizable basin, sift the flour, salt, sugar, baking soda, and baking powder.
3. Mix in the chilled butter until a crumbly texture is achieved.
4. Buttermilk should be slowly incorporated while mixing until dough forms.
5. On a floured surface, roll out the dough to a thickness of 1/2 inch and use a 13/4-inch round cookie cutter to cut out circles.
6. Butter the biscuits and place them in a single layer in a pie pan.
7. Cook for about 8 minutes, or until golden brown, in the air fryer.

Ninja Pop-tarts

PREPARATION TIME REQUIRED	
Coking Time:	1 Hour
Servings:	6

INGREDIENTS TO USE

Lemon Glaze:

1¼ cups powdered swerve

2 tablespoons lemon juice zest of 1 lemon

1 teaspoon coconut oil, melted

¼ teaspoon vanilla extract

Pop-tarts:

tablespoons swerve

2/3 cup very cold coconut oil

½ teaspoon vanilla extract

½ cup of ice-cold water Pop-tarts:

¼ teaspoon salt

cup coconut flour 1 cup almond flour

GOOD STEP BY STEP DIRECTIONS

1. Pop-Tarts: Grease an air fryer basket and heat the air fryer to 375 degrees Fahrenheit.
2. Add the coconut oil after combining all the flour, Swerve, and salt in a bowl.
3. A mixture of almond meals will develop after thoroughly mixing with a fork. Once a solid dough forms, add vanilla and 1 tablespoon of cold water and stir well.
4. Divide the dough in half, then flatten each half out into a thin sheet. Transfer

4 of the rectangles to the Air Fryer basket after cutting each sheet into 12 identically sized rectangles.

5. Cook the remaining rectangles for an additional ten minutes, then repeat.

6. Lemon Glaze: While the tarts are cooking, combine the ingredients for the lemon glaze and drizzle it over them.

7. Add sprinkles, then serve.

Zucchini Brownies

PREPARATION TIME REQUIRED	
Coking Time:	35 minutes
Servings:	12

INGREDIENTS TO USE

¼ teaspoon baking soda 1 egg

1 cup butter

unsweetened 1 teaspoon ground cinnamon

½ teaspoon ground nutmeg

1 cup dark chocolate chips

1½ cups zucchini, shredded

1 teaspoon vanilla extract

1/3 cup applesauce,

GOOD STEP BY STEP DIRECTIONS

1. Grease three sizable ramekins and heat the air fryer to 345 degrees.
2. The ingredients should be thoroughly mixed in a big basin.
3. Pour into the ramekins as evenly as possible, then use a spatula to level the top.
4. Place the ramekin in the Air Fryer basket and cook for 35 minutes approximately.
5. Slice the prepared dish to serve.

Avocado Cake

PREPARATION TIME REQUIRED	
Coking Time:	3 minutes
Servings:	4

INGREDIENTS TO USE

tablespoons butter melted 4 eggs, whisked
teaspoons baking powder 1 cup swerve
4 ounces raspberries
avocados, peeled, pitted
and mashed 1 cup of almonds flour

GOOD STEP BY STEP DIRECTIONS

1. After lining a cake pan that will fit an air fryer with parchment paper, combine all the ingredients in a bowl and stir. Place the pan in the air fryer and cook at 340 degrees F for 30 minutes. Slice and serve the cake after it has had time to cool.

Vanilla Pound Cake

PREPARATION TIME REQUIRED	
Coking Time:	30 minutes
Servings:	12

INGREDIENTS TO USE

2/3 cup butter, melted 4 large eggs
¼ teaspoon salt
½ cup erythritol powder
1 vanilla bean, scraped 1/3 cup water

GOOD STEP BY STEP DIRECTIONS

2. Give the air fryer five minutes to warm up.
3. In a mixing basin, mix all the ingredients.
4. Add to a baking dish that has been buttered.
5. 30 minutes of baking at 375 0F in the air fryer.

Choco-coconut Puddin

PREPARATION TIME REQUIRED	
Coking Time:	65 minutes
Servings:	1

INGREDIENTS TO USE

½ tbsp quality gelatin 1 tbsp water
tbsp cacao powder or organic cocoa
cup coconut milk
½ tsp Sugar powder extract or
2 tbsp honey/maple syrup

GOOD STEP BY STEP DIRECTIONS

1. Combine the coconut milk, cocoa, and sweetener over medium heat.
2. Gelatin and water should be combined in a different bowl.
3. Add to the pan while stirring until everything is dissolved.
4. Place in tiny bowls and chill for an hour.
5. Serve!

Chocolate Molten Lava Cake

PREPARATION TIME REQUIRED	
Coking Time:	25 minutes
Servings:	4

INGREDIENTS TO USE

eggs

3 ½ oz. the chocolate melted 1 ½ tbsp. flour

½ oz. butter

melted 3 ½ tbsp. sugar

GOOD STEP BY STEP DIRECTIONS

1. Heat the Air Fryer to 375 degrees.
2. Four ramekins should be butter-greased.
3. Before adding in the melted chocolate, thoroughly blend the eggs and butter.
4. Fold the flour in gradually.
5. Each ramekin should have an equal amount of the mixture.
6. Cook them for 10 minutes in the air fryer.
7. Let the cakes fall out of the ramekins by turning them over onto plates. Serve warm.

Nuts Cookies

PREPARATION TIME REQUIRED	
Coking Time:	10 minutes
Servings:	6

INGREDIENTS TO USE

½ teaspoon baking powder 3 tablespoons Erythritol Cooking spray

oz macadamia nuts, grinded

½ cup butter softened 1 cup coconut flour

GOOD STEP BY STEP DIRECTIONS

1. Butter, coconut flour, ground coconut nuts, baking powder, and erythritol should all be combined in a mixing bowl. Prepare the dough by kneading it. Roll the dough into balls after cutting it into small pieces. To get the shape of the cookies, lightly press each cookie ball. To 365F, preheat the air fryer. Spray cooking oil on the air fryer basket. In the air fryer, cook the uncooked cookies for 8 minutes. To achieve the light brown crust, heat for an additional 2 minutes at 390F.

Crème Brulee

PREPARATION TIME REQUIRED	
Coking Time:	1 Hour
Servings:	3

INGREDIENTS TO USE

4 tbsp sugar + extra for topping
vanilla pods
cup milk
10 egg yolks

GOOD STEP BY STEP DIRECTIONS

1. Add the milk and cream to a pan. Open the vanilla beans and scrape the seeds into the pan along with the beans. On a stovetop, place the pan and heat it to almost boiling while stirring often. Cut the heat off. Beat the egg yolks after adding them to a bowl. Add the sugar and stir until smooth but not very frothy.
2. After removing the vanilla pods, pour the milk mixture over the egg mixture and stir continually. Allow it to sit for a while. Put the mixture into two to three ramekins. The ramekins should be placed in the fryer basket and cooked for 50 minutes at 190 F. When done, take out the ramekins and allow them to cool. The remaining sugar should be sprinkled on top and melted with a torch so that it browns on top.

Dark Chocolate Brownies

PREPARATION TIME REQUIRED

Coking Time:	35 minutes
Servings:	10

INGREDIENTS TO USE

1 cup chopped walnuts
1 cup white chocolate chips
¾ cup white sugar 3 eggs
2 tsp vanilla extract
¾ cup flour
¼ cup cocoa powder
6 oz butter

GOOD STEP BY STEP DIRECTIONS

1. Use baking paper to line a pan inside your air fryer. Melt chocolate and butter in a saucepan over low heat. Continue to whisk the mixture until it becomes smooth. Whisk in eggs and vanilla after allowing to slightly cool. Sift the flour and cocoa, then stir to combine. Add the white chocolate to the batter after scattering the walnuts on top. Cook the batter for 20 minutes at 340 F after pouring it into the pan. Serve with ice cream and raspberry syrup.

Nutella And Banana Pastries

PREPARATION TIME REQUIRED

Coking Time:	12 minutes
Servings:	4

INGREDIENTS TO USE

bananas, sliced
½ cup Nutella
2 tablespoons icing sugar
puff pastry sheet, cut into 4 equal squares

GOOD STEP BY STEP DIRECTIONS

1. Grease an air fryer basket and preheat the air fryer to 375 degrees Fahrenheit.
2. Each pastry square should be covered in Nutella, then topped with banana slices and icing sugar.

3. Each square should be folded into a triangle, and the corners should be fork-slightly pressed.
4. Place the pastries in the Air Fryer basket and cook for 12 minutes approximately.
5. Remove the dish and serve right away.

Orange Swiss Roll

PREPARATION TIME REQUIRED	
Coking Time:	1H 30Minutes
Servings:	

INGREDIENTS TO USE

cup almond flour 1 cup coconut flour

1/2 cup confectioners' swerve

1/2 cup milk

1/4 cup swerve

1 tablespoon yeast

1/2 stick butter, at room temperature 1 egg, at room temperature

1/4 teaspoon salt

tablespoons fresh orange juice Filling:2 tablespoons butter

4 tablespoons swerve

teaspoon ground star anise 1/4 teaspoon ground cinnamon

1 teaspoon vanilla paste

GOOD STEP BY STEP DIRECTIONS

1. Warm the milk in a microwave-safe bowl before adding it to the bowl of an electric stand mixer. Swerve and yeast should be added, and they should be thoroughly combined. When the yeast is frothy, cover it and let it settle.
2. The butter should then be whipped at a low speed. Add the egg after mixing once more. Add flour and salt. When a soft dough develops, add the orange juice and continue to mix at medium speed.
3. The dough should be kneaded on a lightly dusted surface. Loosely cover it and let it in a warm area for approximately an hour, or until it has doubled in size. Next, spray cooking oil on the sides and bottom of a baking pan (butter flavored).
4. Your dough should be rolled into a rectangle.
5. 2 tablespoons of butter should be applied evenly to the dough. Sprinkle the dough with the mixture of 4 tablespoons of swerve, ground star anise, cinnamon, and vanilla.

6. Make a log out of your dough by rolling it up. Place them in the Air Fryer basket lined with parchment after cutting them into equal rolls.

7. 12 minutes of baking at 350 degrees during which they were turned once. Sprinkle with confectioners' sugar, then relish!

Egg Custard

PREPARATION TIME REQUIRED	
Coking Time:	33 Minutes
Servings:	6

INGREDIENTS TO USE

2 cups heavy whipping cream 1/2 tsp vanilla
eggs
1/2 cup erythritol
1 tsp nutmeg
egg yolks

GOOD STEP BY STEP DIRECTIONS

1. Set the air fryer's temperature to 325 F.
2. Beat all of the ingredients together in a large bowl after adding them.
3. Put the oiled baking dish with the custard mixture inside the air fryer.
4. For 32 minutes, cook.
5. Place it in the refrigerator for a minimum of one to two hours after fully cooling.
6. Enjoy after serving.

Creamy Rice Pudding

PREPARATION TIME REQUIRED	
Coking Time:	20 Minutes
Servings:	6

INGREDIENTS TO USE

1 tablespoon heavy cream 1 teaspoon vanilla extract
16 ounces milk 1/3 cup sugar
 1 tablespoon butter, melted 7 ounces white rice

GOOD STEP BY STEP DIRECTIONS

1. In a pan that will fit your air fryer, combine all the ingredients and stir well.
2. Place the pan in the fryer and cook it for minutes at 360 degrees Fahrenheit.
3. The pudding should be stirred, divided into bowls,
4. and served chilled.

Peach Parcel

PREPARATION TIME REQUIRED

Coking Time:	15 Minutes
Servings:	2

INGREDIENTS TO USE

beaten lightly 1 tablespoon sugar
Pinch of ground cinnamon
1 tablespoon whipped cream
puff pastry sheets 1 egg,
peach, peeled, cored
and halved 1 cup of prepared vanilla custard

GOOD STEP BY STEP DIRECTIONS

1. Grease an air fryer basket and preheat the air fryer to 340 degrees Fahrenheit.
2. Each pastry sheet should include a peach half and a tablespoon of vanilla custard in the middle.
3. Sprinkle the cinnamon and sugar mixture over the peach halves.
4. Form a parcel out of the sheets by pinching their corners together, then place it in the air fryer basket.
5. Cook for about a minute, then add whipped cream on top.
6. Remove from dish and top with remaining custard.

Vanilla Coconut Cheese Cookies

PREPARATION TIME REQUIRED

Coking Time:	12 Minutes
Servings:	15

INGREDIENTS TO USE

3 tbsp cream cheese, softened 1/2 cup coconut flour
Pinch of salt
1/2 cup butter, softened
1/2 tsp baking powder 1 tsp vanilla
1 egg

1/2 cup swerve

GOOD STEP BY STEP DIRECTIONS

1. Cream cheese, butter, and sweetener should be combined in a bowl.
2. Beat until smooth and creamy after adding the egg and vanilla.
3. Mix in the baking powder, salt, and coconut flour after adding them. For one hour, cover and place in the refrigerator.
4. Set the air fryer's temperature to 325 F.
5. Create cookies from the dough, and heat for 12 minutes in the air fryer.
6. Enjoy after serving.

Mom's Orange Rolls

PREPARATION TIME REQUIRED	
Coking Time:	1 Hour 20 Minutes
Servings:	6

INGREDIENTS TO USE

1/2 stick butter, at room temperature 1 egg, at room temperature

2 tablespoons fresh orange juice Filling:

1/4 teaspoon salt

1/2 cup milk

1/4 cup granulated sugar 1 tablespoon yeast

2 cups all-purpose flour

2 tablespoons butter

4 tablespoons white sugar

1/2 cup confectioners' sugar

teaspoon ground star anise

1/4 teaspoon ground cinnamon

1 teaspoon vanilla paste

GOOD STEP BY STEP DIRECTIONS

1. Warm the milk in a microwave-safe bowl before adding it to the bowl of an electric stand mixer. Mix well before adding the yeast and granulated sugar. When the yeast is frothy, cover it and let it settle.

2. The butter should then be whipped at a low speed. Add the egg after mixing once more. Add flour and salt. When a soft dough develops, add the orange juice and continue to mix at medium speed.

3. The dough should be kneaded on a lightly dusted surface. Loosely cover it and let it in a warm area for approximately an hour, or until it has doubled in size. Then, spritz cooking oil (preferably butter-flavored) on the bottom and edges of a baking pan.

4. Your dough should be rolled into a rectangle.

5. 2 tablespoons of butter should be applied evenly to the dough. White sugar, ground star anise, cinnamon, and vanilla should be combined in a mixing bowl and distributed equally over the dough.

6. Make a log out of your dough by rolling it up. Place them in the Air Fryer basket lined with parchment after cutting them into equal rolls.

7. 12 minutes of baking at 350 degrees during which they were turned once. Sprinkle with confectioners' sugar, then relish!

Vanilla Mozzarella Balls

PREPARATION TIME REQUIRED	
Coking Time:	**4 Minutes**
Servings:	8

INGREDIENTS TO USE

2 tablespoons swerve
teaspoon almond butter melted 7 oz coconut flour
oz almond flour
½ teaspoon vanilla extract cooking spray
eggs, beaten
5 oz Mozzarella, shredded 1 tablespoon butter
1 teaspoon baking powder

GOOD STEP BY STEP DIRECTIONS

1. Combine the butter and mozzarella in a mixing bowl. Melt the mixture in the microwave for 15 minutes. Add coconut flour and almond flour next. Add baking powder and Swerve.
2. Add vanilla extract next, then whisk the mixture. Work the tender dough. If the mixture is not sufficiently melted, microwave it for another 2 to 5 seconds. Combine almond butter and eggs in the bowl.
3. From the almond flour mixture, form 8 balls and then dip them in the egg mixture. Set the air fryer to 400F for frying. Place the bread rolls in a single layer inside the air fryer basket after spraying it with cooking spray from the inside. For 4 minutes, or until the bread roll is golden brown, bake the dessert. If desired, add Splenda after completely cooling the prepared dessert.

Peach Slices

PREPARATION TIME REQUIRED	
Coking Time:	**40 Minutes**
Servings:	4

INGREDIENTS TO USE

4 cups peaches, sliced 2 – 3 tbsp. sugar

⅓ cup oats

2 tbsp. unsalted butter

¼ tsp. vanilla extract 1 tsp. cinnamon

2 tbsp. flour

GOOD STEP BY STEP DIRECTIONS

1. Sliced peaches, sugar, vanilla extract, and cinnamon should all be combined in a big basin. Put the mixture in an air fryer after pouring it into a baking pan.
2. Cook at 290°F for minutes.
3. Oats, flour, and unsalted butter should be mixed in a separate basin while you wait.
4. Pour the butter mixture on top of the cooked peach slices.
5. Cook at 300-310°F for a further 10 minutes.
6. Take out of the fryer and let the food crisp up for 5 to 10 minutes. If preferred, serve with ice cream.

Butter Crumble

PREPARATION TIME REQUIRED	
Coking Time:	25 Minutes
Servings:	4

INGREDIENTS TO USE

1 tablespoon cream cheese 1 teaspoon baking powder
tablespoons butter, softened 2 tablespoons Erythritol
oz peanuts, crushed
½ teaspoon lemon juice
½ cup coconut flour

GOOD STEP BY STEP DIRECTIONS

1. Combine the coconut flour, butter, erythritol, baking soda, and lemon juice in a mixing bowl. The mixture should be thoroughly mixed. After that, freeze it for a few minutes. Combine cream cheese and peanuts in the meanwhile. Grate the ice cream dough. Use baking paper to line the air fryer molds. Then,
2. place half of the grated dough in the mold and press it flat. Add a cream cheese mixture on top. After that, sprinkle the leftover dough over the cream cheese mixture.
3. Place the crumble mold in the air fryer, and cook it at 330F for 25 minutes.

White Chocolate Berry Cheesecake

PREPARATION TIME REQUIRED	
Coking Time:	5 -10 Minutes
Servings:	4

INGREDIENTS TO USE

1 tsp raspberries
½ tsp Splenda
1 tbsp Da Vinci Sugar-Free syrup, white chocolate flavor
8 oz cream cheese, softened 2 oz heavy cream

GOOD STEP BY STEP DIRECTIONS

1. Blend the ingredients until they are thick.
2. Pour into mugs.
3. Refrigerate.
4. Serve!

Coconut Strawberry Fritters

PREPARATION TIME REQUIRED	
Coking Time:	15 Minutes
Servings:	8

INGREDIENTS TO USE

1/2 teaspoon coconut extract 1/2 teaspoon baking powder 3/4 cup all-purpose flour
3/4-pound strawberries
1/3 cup demerara sugar
1/8 teaspoon salt1 ¼ cups soy milk
3 tablespoons coconut oil

GOOD STEP BY STEP DIRECTIONS

1. In a mixing bowl, thoroughly combine all the ingredients.
2. The mixture is then poured into the frying basket of the air fryer and air-fried for 4 minutes at 345 degrees Fahrenheit.
3. If desired, sprinkle with ginger sugar.
4. Good appetite!

Classic White Chocolate Cookies

PREPARATION TIME REQUIRED	
Coking Time:	40 Minutes
Servings:	10

INGREDIENTS TO USE

1. 6/3 cups of butter
2. A third cup of almond flour Coconut flour, 1/2 cup; coconut oil, tbsp Granulated swerve in 3/4 cup
3. 1/3 teaspoon of star anise allspice, ground, 13 teaspoons grated nutmeg, 1/3 teaspoon 1/four teaspoon of sea salt, fine
4. Unsweetened white chocolate weighing 8 ounces and two well-beaten eggs

GOOD STEP BY STEP DIRECTIONS

1. Place all of the ingredients listed above in a mixing bowl, excluding the egg. Then, use your hands to knead the dough until it becomes soft. Place for 20 minutes in the refrigerator. Make small balls out of the refrigerated dough, flatten them, and heat the air fryer to 350 degrees Fahrenheit.
2. Use the last of the egg to create an egg wash. After baking the cookies for around 11 minutes, glaze them with egg wash. Good appetite!

Lemon Glazed Muffins

PREPARATION TIME REQUIRED	
Coking Time:	30 Minutes
Servings:	6

INGREDIENTS TO USE

tbsp vegetable oil
½ cup milk
½ cup sugar 1 small egg
tsp lemon zest
½ tsp vanilla extract Glaze:
¾ tsp baking powder
¼ tsp baking soda
½ tsp salt
½ cup powdered sugar 2 tsp lemon juice

GOOD STEP BY STEP DIRECTIONS

1. Set the air fryer to 350 degrees. In a bowl, combine the dry ingredients for the muffin. The wet components should be whisked together in another bowl. Combine the two ingredients gently. Six muffin pans with oil should receive the batter.
2. In the air fryer, put the muffin tins, and cook for 1 to 14 minutes. Lemon juice and powdered sugar are whisked together. The muffins are covered with the glaze.

Apple Bread Pudding

PREPARATION TIME REQUIRED

Coking Time:	44 Minutes
Servings:	8

INGREDIENTS TO USE

1/3 cup plain flour 3/5 cup brown sugar 7 tablespoons butter

For Bread Pudding:

5 tablespoons honey

2 teaspoons ground cinnamon 2 teaspoons cornstarch

1 teaspoon vanilla extract For Topping:

10½ ounces bread, cubed

½ cup apple, peeled, cored, and chopped

½ cup raisins

¼ cup walnuts, chopped 1½ cups milk

¾ cup water

GOOD STEP BY STEP DIRECTIONS

1. Mix the bread, apple, raisins, and walnuts thoroughly in a large bowl.
2. The remaining pudding ingredients should be mixed thoroughly in a separate bowl.
3. Mix well after adding the milk mixture to the bread mixture.
4. Refrigerate for approximately 15 minutes while occasionally tossing.
5. The flour and sugar should be combined in a bowl for the topping.
6. Add the butter and blend with a pastry cutter until a crumbly mixture forms.
7. Set the air fryer to 355 degrees Fahrenheit.
8. Spread the topping mixture over each of the two baking pans after evenly dividing the mixture between them.
9. One pan should fit within the air fryer basket.
10. For around 22 minutes, air fry.
11. Continue with the second pan.
12. Serve warm after removing from the air fryer.

Blueberry Pancakes

PREPARATION TIME REQUIRED

Coking Time:	20 Minutes
Servings:	4

INGREDIENTS TO USE

eggs, beaten
½ tsp. vanilla extract 2 tbsp. honey
½ cup blueberries
½ cup sugar
cups + 2 tbsp. flour
1 cup milk
1 tsp. baking powder Pinch of salt

GOOD STEP BY STEP DIRECTIONS

1. Set the Air Fryer to 390°F in advance.
2. Combine all of the dry ingredients in a bowl.
3. The wet components should be added and whisked together to create a smooth mixture.
4. Before mixing them into the mixture, lightly dust each blueberry with flour. This is to make sure the batter doesn't change color.
5. Put a little oil or butter into the baking dish.
6. Place numerous equal portions of the batter in pancake-like shapes on the baking sheet, making sure to leave plenty of space between each one. It might be necessary to finish this in two batches.
7. Bake the dish for about 10 minutes after placing it in the oven.

Lemon Curd

PREPARATION TIME REQUIRED	
Coking Time:	30 Minutes
Servings:	2

INGREDIENTS TO USE

3 tbsp sugar
¾ lemon, juiced
1 egg
1 egg yolk

GOOD STEP BY STEP DIRECTIONS

1. In a medium ramekin, evenly combine the butter and sugar. Egg and yolk should

be added gradually while continuing to stir to achieve a bright yellow color. Lemon juice is added; combine. Cook the bowl for 6 minutes at 250 F in the fryer basket. Cook for a few minutes at a temperature increase to 320 F.

2. Use a spoon to examine for lumps and then flip the bowl over onto a level surface. Refrigerate the ramekin overnight or serve it right away. Cover with plastic wrap.

Coconut Chip Cookies

PREPARATION TIME REQUIRED	
Coking Time:	20 Minutes
Servings:	12

INGREDIENTS TO USE

2 cups coconut chips

tablespoons coconut milk 1 teaspoon of coconut extract 1 teaspoon of vanilla extract

2 ¼ cups all-purpose flour

1/2 teaspoon baking powder

1/2 teaspoon baking soda 1/2 teaspoon fine table salt

¾ cups granulated sugar 3 eggs

1 cup butter, melted

GOOD STEP BY STEP DIRECTIONS

1. Set your Air Fryer to 350 degrees Fahrenheit to start. Beat the butter and sugar together thoroughly in the bowl of an electric mixer. At this point, add each egg one at a time and thoroughly combine. Next, add the coconut milk, coconut extract, and vanilla and beat until smooth and creamy.

2. Salt, baking soda, and baking powder are combined with the flour. Once everything is thoroughly combined, add the flour mixture to the butter mixture and whisk again.

3. Add the coconut chips last, then stir one more. Scoop out 1 tablespoon-sized ball of the batter and place them two inches apart on a baking sheet.

4. Rotate the pan once or twice during the cooking process and bake for 10 minutes, or until golden brown.

5. Cookies should cool on wire racks. Good appetite!

Almond Bars

PREPARATION TIME REQUIRED

Coking Time: 35 Minutes
Servings: 12

INGREDIENTS TO USE

¾ cup cherries pitted 1 ½ cup almond flour 1 tbsp xanthan gum
½ cup butter softened ½ tsp salt
2 eggs, lightly beaten 1 cup erythritol
½ tsp vanilla
¼ cup water

GOOD STEP BY STEP DIRECTIONS

1. Almond flour, erythritol, eggs, vanilla, butter, and salt should all be combined in a bowl to form a dough.
2. Baked dough in an air fryer, and press down.
3. Cook for 10 minutes at 5 F in the air fryer.
4. Cherries, xanthan gum, and water should be combined in the meantime.
5. Pour cherry mixture over heated dough and continue cooking for an additional 2 minutes.
6. Slice, then dish.

Rustic Baked Apples

PREPARATION TIME REQUIRED

Coking Time: 25 Minutes
Servings: 4

INGREDIENTS TO USE

1/4 cup rolled oats 1/4 cup sugar
4 Gala apples
2/3 cup water
2 tablespoons honey
1/3 cup walnuts, chopped
1 teaspoon cinnamon powder
1/2 teaspoon ground cardamom 1/2 teaspoon ground cloves

GOOD STEP BY STEP DIRECTIONS

1. Making deep holes in the apples, cut out the stem and seeds with a paring knife.
2. Rolling oats, sugar, honey, walnuts, cinnamon, cardamom, and cloves should all be combined in a mixing basin.
3. In a dish suitable for an air fryer, pour the water. Add the apples to the serving dish.
4. 17 minutes of baking at 3 F. At room temperature, serve. Good appetite!

Banana Split

PREPARATION TIME REQUIRED	
Coking Time:	10 Minutes
Servings:	8

INGREDIENTS TO USE

½ cup corn flour 2 eggs

1 cup panko bread crumbs

tablespoons sugar

¼ teaspoon ground cinnamon

4 bananas, peeled and halved lengthwise

tablespoons walnuts, chopped 3 tablespoons coconut oil

GOOD STEP BY STEP DIRECTIONS

1. Lightly grease an air fryer basket and preheat the air fryer to 280 degrees Fahrenheit.
2. In a skillet over medium heat, add bread crumbs and coconut oil.
3. Transfer to a bowl after cooking for 4 minutes until golden brown.
4. In one shallow dish, add the flour, and in another shallow dish, beat the eggs.
5. Slices of banana should be equally covered in flour, then dipped in eggs, and then again in bread crumbs.
6. Sprinkle the banana slices with the sugar and cinnamon mixture that you made in a small bowl.
7. Banana slices should be arranged in the Air Fryer basket and cooked for approximately 10 minutes.
8. Add walnuts on top, then serve.

Greek-style Griddle Cakes

PREPARATION TIME REQUIRED	
Coking Time:	15 Minutes
Servings:	4

INGREDIENTS TO USE

2 eggs, lightly beaten 1 tablespoon butter
3/4 cup self-rising flour
1/4 teaspoon fine sea salt
2 tablespoons sugar
1/2 cup milk
Topping:
tablespoons honey
cup Greek-style yogurt 1 banana, mashed

GOOD STEP BY STEP DIRECTIONS

1. In a bowl, combine the sugar, salt, and flour. Add the milk, eggs, and butter after that. Blend until homogeneous and smooth.
2. Toppings of the batter should be dropped into the Air Fryer pan.
3. Cook the griddle cakes at 0 degrees F for 4 to 5 minutes, or until bubbles start to appear on their surface. Continue by using the remaining batter.
4. Mix all of the topping ingredients while waiting. Place there until you're ready to serve, then refrigerate. Serve the cold topping alongside the griddle cakes. Enjoy!

Cashew Pie

PREPARATION TIME REQUIRED	
Coking Time:	18 Minutes
Servings:	8

INGREDIENTS TO USE

½ tsp baking soda 1/3 cup heavy cream
egg
oz cashews, crushed
1 oz dark chocolate, melted 1 tbsp butter
1 tsp vinegar
1 cup coconut flour

GOOD STEP BY STEP DIRECTIONS

1. Egg should be added to a bowl and beat with a hand mixer. Stir in the coconut flour thoroughly.
2. Stir in the melted chocolate, heavy cream, vinegar, baking soda, and butter.
3. Mix in the cashews well.
4. Set the air fryer to 350 degrees.
5. Place the prepared dough in the baking dish for the air fryer and form it into a pie.
6. For 18 minutes, cook.
7. Slice, then dish.

Ricotta And Lemon Cake Recipe

PREPARATION TIME REQUIRED	
Coking Time:	1 Hour 10 Minutes
Servings:	4

INGREDIENTS TO USE

Zest from 1 lemon; grated Zest from 1 orange;
grated 1/2 lb. sugar
8 eggs; whisked
3 lbs. ricotta cheese
Butter for the pan

GOOD STEP BY STEP DIRECTIONS

1. Eggs should be thoroughly combined with sugar, cheese, lemon, and orange zest in a bowl.
2. Bake for 30 minutes at 390 °F in an air fryer-compatible baking pan that has been greased with batter and ricotta mixture.
3. 40 more minutes of baking are required at 0 °F reduced heat. Take the cake out of the oven, let it cool, then serve!

THANK YOU FOR READING THIS BOOK

Printed in Great Britain
by Amazon

46862726R00079